CLASSROOM
ASSESSMENT & GRADING
that Work

Robert J. Marzano

Association for Supervision and Curriculum Development ◆ Alexandria, Virginia USA

Association for Supervision and Curriculum Development
1703 N. Beauregard St. • Alexandria, VA 22311-1714 USA
Phone: 800-933-2723 or 703-578-9600 • Fax: 703-575-5400
Web site: www.ascd.org • E-mail: member@ascd.org
Author guidelines: www.ascd.org/write

Gene R. Carter, *Executive Director;* Nancy Modrak, *Director of Publishing;* Julie Houtz, *Director of Book Editing & Production;* Darcie Russell, *Project Manager;* Georgia Park, *Senior Graphic Designer;* Barton, Matheson, Willse & Worthington, *Typesetter;* Vivian Coss, *Production Specialist*

Printed in the United States of America. Cover art copyright © 2006 by ASCD. ASCD publications present a variety of viewpoints. The views expressed or implied in this book should not be interpreted as official positions of the Association.

All Web links in this book are correct as of the publication date below but may have become inactive or otherwise modified since that time. If you notice a deactivated or changed link, please e-mail books@ascd.org with the words "Link Update" in the subject line. In your message, please specify the Web link, the book title, and the page number on which the link appears.

PAPERBACK ISBN-13: 978-1-4166-0422-8   ASCD product #106006   s12/06
PAPERBACK ISBN-10: 1-4166-0422-7
Also available as an e-book through ebrary, netLibrary, and many online booksellers
(see Books in Print for the ISBNs).

Quantity discounts for the paperback edition only: 10–49 copies, 10%; 50+ copies, 15%; for 1,000 or more copies, call 800-933-2723, ext. 5634, or 703-575-5634. For desk copies: member@ascd.org.

Library of Congress Cataloging-in-Publication Data
Marzano, Robert J.
    Classroom assessment and grading that work / Robert J. Marzano.
        p.   cm.
    Includes bibliographical references and index.
    ISBN-13: 978-1-4166-0422-8 (pbk. : alk. paper)
    ISBN-10: 1-4166-0422-7 (pbk. : alk. paper)   1. Educational tests and measurements—United States.   2. Grading and marking (Students)—United States.   3. Examinations—Design and construction.   I. Association for Supervision and Curriculum Development.   II. Title.
    LB3051.M4573 2006
    371.27—dc22
                                                                            2006020642

18 17 16 15 14 13 12 11 10 09 08 07   2 3 4 5 6 7 8 9 10 11 12

This book is dedicated

to Cliff Nolte:

- Father-in-law
- Friend
- Teacher

CLASSROOM ASSESSMENT & GRADING *that* Work

LIST OF FIGURES

1

The Case for
Classroom Assessment

Improving the academic achievement of K–12 students has been a central concern of educators in the United States since at least the early 1890s, when leaders of industry, politicians, parents, and the society at large realized that an educated populus was the closest thing a country could have to a guarantee of a bright future (Ravitch, 1983). Since that time, a wide array of educational innovations have been tried, all of which were designed to enhance student achievement. Educators have experimented with such things as changing the schedule, decreasing the student-to-teacher ratio, increasing the availability and use of technology, and so on. All of these innovations have merit. However, not even the best has demonstrated the impact on student achievement of the most intuitively important variable in the educational system—the classroom teacher.

Virtually every study that has examined the role of the classroom teacher in the process of educating students has come to the same straightforward conclusion: an effective teacher enhances student learning more than any other aspect of schooling that can be controlled. To illustrate, after analyzing test scores of more than 60,000 students across grades 3 through 5, researchers S. Paul Wright, Sandra Horn, and William Sanders (1997) made the following observation:

> The results of this study will document that the most important factor affecting student learning is the teacher. In addition, the results show wide variation in effectiveness among teachers. The immediate and clear implication of this finding is that seemingly more can be done to improve education by improving the effectiveness of teachers than by any other single factor. Effective teachers appear to be effective with students of all achievement levels, regardless of the level of heterogeneity in their classrooms. If the teacher is ineffective, students under the teacher's tutelage will

show inadequate progress academically regardless of how similar or different they are regarding their academic achievement. (p. 63)

Other studies have corroborated the conclusions of Wright, Horn, and Sanders (for a review of other studies, see Nye, Konstantopoulos, & Hedges, 2004). Kati Haycock (1998) dramatizes the effect of a classroom teacher by comparing what one can expect from a student spending a year with the "most effective teacher" and the "least effective teacher" (for a discussion of how "most effective" and "least effective" teachers are defined, see Technical Note 1.1). Haycock explains that the most effective teacher produces an achievement gain of 52 percentile points in student achievement, whereas the least effective teacher produces a gain of only 14 percentile points—a difference of 38 percentile points. This finding is made even more dramatic when one realizes that it has been estimated that students gain about 6 percentile points in academic achievement simply from growing one year older and gleaning new knowledge and skill from daily life (Cahen & Davis, 1987; Hattie, 1992). The ineffective teacher adds little more than life experience.

Given the potentially strong and positive effect of a classroom teacher, a logical question is, what do highly effective teachers do? Again, many answers have been proposed, most of which focus on lists of instructional and management strategies (see Hattie, 1992; Marzano, Marzano, & Pickering, 2003; Marzano, Pickering, & Pollock, 2001). These lists emphasize the use of strategies such as well-designed practice activities, comparison activities, communicating learning goals, and using pictures, graphs, and pictographs to represent knowledge. Although it is certainly true that "high-yield" instructional strategies and classroom management strategies are a critical part of effective teaching, this book is about one aspect of teaching that is frequently overlooked in discussions of ways to enhance student achievement: classroom assessment.

To the surprise of some educators, major reviews of the research on the effects of classroom assessment indicate that it might be one of the most powerful weapons in a teacher's arsenal. To illustrate, as a result of a synthesis of more than 250 studies, Paul Black and Dylan Wiliam (1998) describe the impact of effective classroom assessment in the following way:

> The research reported here shows conclusively that formative assessment does improve learning. The gains in achievement appear to be quite considerable, and as noted earlier, amongst the largest ever reported for educational interventions. As an illustration of just how big these gains are, an effect size of 0.7 [see Technical Note 1.2 for a description of an effect size], if it could be achieved on a nationwide scale, would be equivalent to raising the mathematics attainment score of an "average"

country like England, New Zealand or the United States into the "top five" after the Pacific rim countries of Singapore, Korea, Japan and Hong Kong. (p. 61)

It is important to note that Black and Wiliam's (1998) comments address formative as opposed to summative assessments. This distinction is addressed in the next section. To get a sense of Black and Wiliam's conclusions, consider Figure 1.1 (see Technical Note 1.3 for a description of how Figure 1.1 was derived). The upper part of Figure 1.1 depicts a teacher who begins at the 50th percentile in terms of her skill at using classroom assessments and a student in her class who begins at the 50th percentile in terms of his achievement. Over time the teacher increases her effectiveness at using classroom assessment to the 84th percentile. Given Black and Wiliam's findings, one would predict that the student's achievement would increase to the 63rd percentile. The lower part of Figure 1.1 represents an even more dramatic scenario. If the teacher increases from the 50th to the 99th percentile in terms of skill at using classroom assessments, one would predict the student's achievement to increase to the 78th percentile.

At face value, the findings reported in Figure 1.1 are remarkable—classroom assessment can have a dramatic influence on student achievement. Given these findings, one might be tempted to conclude that assessing students more will automatically increase their learning. Such a conclusion would be wrong. Like most things in education, classroom assessment enhances student achievement under certain conditions only. Fortunately, the research provides some guidance regarding those conditions.

A Brief Review of the Research on Classroom Assessment

Scholars have conducted many reviews of the research on classroom assessment. Some of the more comprehensive reviews are those by Natriello (1987); Fuchs and Fuchs (1986); Crooks (1988); Bangert-Drowns, Kulik, and Kulik (1991); Bangert-Drowns, Kulik, Kulik, and Morgan (1991); Kluger and DeNisi (1996); and Black and Wiliam (1998). The reviews lead to many conclusions that provide insights into effective classroom assessment; however, four generalizations are particularly germane to this book:

• Feedback from classroom assessments should give students a clear picture of their progress on learning goals and how they might improve.
• Feedback on classroom assessments should encourage students to improve.
• Classroom assessment should be formative in nature.
• Formative classroom assessments should be frequent.

FIGURE 1.1
Effect of Teacher's Increased Skill in Classroom Assessment on Student Achievement

Predicted increase in student achievement when teacher's skill in classroom assessment increases from 50th to 84th percentile.

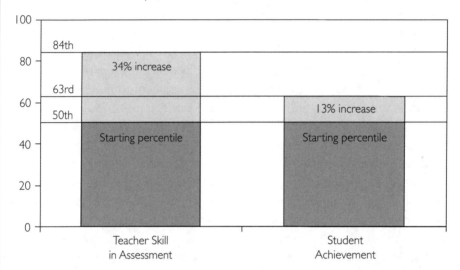

Predicted increase in student achievement when teacher's skill in classroom assessment increases from 50th to 99th percentile.

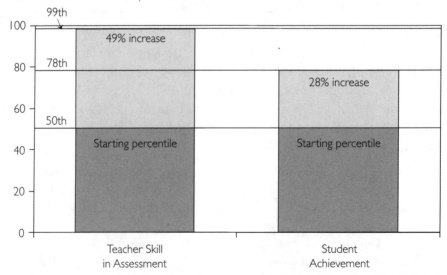

FIGURE 1.2
Findings on the Effects of Different Types of Feedback

Source	Characteristics of Feedback from Classroom Assessment	Number of Studies*	Effect Size	Percentile Gain or Loss in Student Achievement
Bangert-Drowns, Kulik, Kulik, & Morgan (1991)	Right/wrong	6	−.08	−3
	Provide correct answer	39	.22	8.5
	Criteria understood by students vs. not understood	30	.41	16
	Explain	9	.53	20
	Repeat until correct	4	.53	20
Fuchs & Fuchs (1986)	Displaying results graphically	89	.70	26
	Evaluation (interpretation) by rule	49	.91	32

*Indicates the number of studies that were examined by the researchers to compute an effect size. See Technical Note 1.2 for discussion of an effect size.

Providing a Clear Picture of Progress and How to Improve

At a basic level, classroom assessment is a form of feedback to students regarding their progress, and it stands to reason that feedback will enhance learning. Indeed, as a result of reviewing almost 8,000 studies, researcher John Hattie (1992) made the following comment: "The most powerful single modification that enhances achievement is feedback. The simplest prescription for improving education must be 'dollops of feedback' " (p. 9).

As compelling as Hattie's comments are, all forms of feedback are not equally effective. In fact, some forms of feedback might work against learning. To illustrate, consider the research findings depicted in Figure 1.2. The figure presents findings from two major meta-analytic studies—one by Robert Bangert-Drowns, Chen-Lin Kulik, James Kulik, and Mary Teresa Morgan (1991), which reviewed 40 studies on classroom assessment; and one by Lynn Fuchs and Douglas Fuchs (1986), which reviewed 21 studies of assessment. The findings from these two synthesis studies as depicted in Figure 1.2 help one understand this first principle of effective classroom assessment.

Consider the first five rows of Figure 1.2, from the Bangert-Drowns, Kulik, Kulik, and Morgan synthesis. Row 1 indicates that when students receive feedback on a classroom assessment that simply tells them whether their answers are correct or incorrect, learning is negatively influenced. This finding is illustrated by the loss of 3 percentile points. However, when students are provided with the correct answer, learning is influenced in a positive direction. This practice is associated with a gain of 8.5 percentile points in student achievement, as shown in Row 2.

Row 3 of Figure 1.2 addresses whether students are clear about the criteria used to judge their responses. Clarity regarding scoring criteria is associated with a gain of 16 percentile points in student achievement. Row 4 reports a particularly interesting finding—providing students with explanations as to why their responses are correct or incorrect is associated with a gain of 20 percentile points in student achievement. Finally, Row 5 indicates that asking students to continue responding to an assessment until they correctly answer the items is associated with a gain of 20 percentile points.

Rows 6 and 7 of Figure 1.2 are from the Fuchs and Fuchs (1986) study. Row 6 shows the effect of graphically displaying student results. As we shall see in subsequent chapters, displaying assessment results graphically can go a long way to helping students take control of their own learning. However, this practice can also help teachers more accurately judge students' levels of understanding and skill, and it is associated with a gain of 26 percentile points in student achievement. Presumably, seeing a graphic representation of students' scores provides teachers with a more precise and specific frame of reference for making decisions about next instructional steps. Finally, Row 7 addresses the manner in which the teacher interprets assessment results. If the interpretation is done by a set of "rules," student achievement is enhanced by 32 percentile points. In Chapter 3 we will consider this issue in depth. Briefly, though, this finding implies that teachers within a school or a district should have rigorous and uniform ways of interpreting the results of classroom assessments.

Encouraging Students to Improve

One perplexing finding from the research literature is that the manner in which feedback is communicated to students greatly affects whether it has a positive or a negative effect on student achievement. This was one of the major conclusions of a meta-analysis conducted by Avraham Kluger and Angelo DeNisi (1996). After analyzing 607 experimental/control comparisons involving some 23,000 students, the researchers found that in 33 percent of the studies they examined, feedback had a negative impact on achievement. One causal factor they identified for this paradoxical effect is whether feedback encourages or discourages students. To illustrate, Kluger and DeNisi found that when assessment feedback is discouraging to students, it has an effect size of *negative* .14. This translates into a *decrease* in student achievement of 5.5 percentile points (see Technical Note 1.2 for a discussion of effect sizes).

Of course, the critical question that emerges from this finding is, what constitutes encouraging versus discouraging feedback? Kluger and DeNisi warn that this question has no simple answers, but the research provides some strong guidance. To understand the dynamics of encouraging versus discouraging feedback, we must consider two foundational aspects of motivation theory—drive theory and attribution theory.

Drive theory postulates that much of human motivation can be explained as a function of two competing forces, or drives—the striving for success and the fear of failure (Atkinson, 1957, 1964, 1987; Atkinson & Raynor, 1974). Over time, people develop tendencies toward one drive or the other—to be either *success oriented* or *failure avoidant*. When these tendencies become habituated, they translate into strong expectations regarding new tasks—particularly tasks that are challenging to a student.

Success-oriented students tend to be encouraged by challenges because they anticipate the positive feelings that accompany success. Failure-avoidant students tend to be discouraged by challenges because they anticipate the negative feelings that accompany failure. In fact, failure-avoidant students might use self-handicapping strategies that ensure they fail for reasons other than lack of ability. These strategies include procrastination (Rothblum, Solomon, & Murakami, 1986; Solomon & Rothblum, 1984), setting unattainable goals so that failure is ensured (Snyder, 1984), and admitting to small weaknesses or handicaps to establish an excuse for failing—establishing an "academic wooden leg" (Covington, 1992; Covington, Omelich, & Schwarzer, 1986).

Attribution theory provides another perspective on encouraging versus discouraging feedback. It postulates that the manner in which students explain or attribute failure and success encourages or discourages them (Weiner, 1972, 1974; Weiner et al., 1971). In general, individuals attribute their success to four causes: ability, effort, luck, and task difficulty. Of these, the attribution of effort provides the most encouragement. As Martin Covington (1992) explains:

> One of the most important features of attribution theory is its focus on the role of effort in achievement. This emphasis is justified for several reasons. For one thing, if students believe their failures occur for a lack of trying, then they are more likely to remain optimistic about succeeding in the future. For another thing, trying hard is known to increase pride in success and to offset feelings of guilt at having failed. And, perhaps most important of all, the emphasis on the role of effort in achievement is justified because it is widely believed that student effort is modifiable through the actions of teachers. (p. 16)

A fairly straightforward relationship exists between attribution theory and drive theory. Specifically, students who tend to be success oriented also tend to believe in the effort attribution. They perceive that working hard will bring them success. Thus they have a way to succeed, even when faced with challenging tasks. One of the more encouraging aspects of attribution theory is that students who do not believe their efforts produce success can learn over time that they do. Martin Seligman (Seligman, 1975; Seligman, Maier, & Greer, 1968) postulates that students can even cultivate an "explanatory style" that is effort oriented, if they have enough direct experience that effort produces success. Seligman refers to this dynamic as "learned optimism."

Drive theory and attribution theory provide plausible explanations as to why assessment feedback might be encouraging to some students and discouraging to others. Assume that a student has done poorly on an assessment. If the student is failure avoidant, the negative outcome will strengthen the student's belief that he cannot succeed at challenging tasks and the negative feelings associated with such tasks. This combination will most likely discourage the student. However, if the student is success oriented, poor performance on the test will not be as discouraging because the student has a strategy for improvement—to work harder.

In short, drive theory tells us that classroom assessment that is encouraging must have two characteristics. First, teachers must provide students with a way to interpret even low scores in a manner that does not imply failure. If not, failure-avoidant students will continually be discouraged when they do not receive high scores. Second, teachers must provide students with evidence that effort on their part results in higher scores.

The Value of Formative Versus Summative Assessments

The terms *formative* and *summative* are frequently used in discussions of educational assessments. Actually, the concepts of formative and summative assessment when first developed had little to do with classroom assessment or even with learning.

The distinction between formative and summative assessment was first popularized by Michael Scriven in 1967 as part of an American Educational Research Association monograph series on evaluation. Scriven's original point was that a distinction should be made between programs that are being formulated versus programs that have evolved to their final state. Consequently, evaluation takes on different characteristics and is interpreted differently in formative versus summative situations. This distinction was soon applied to the assessment of students. Specifically, *formative assessment* was defined as occurring while knowledge is being learned. *Summative assessment* was defined as occurring at the end of a learning episode—for example, at the end of a course (see McMillan, 2000). More formally,

Peter Airasian (1994) defines formative assessments as those that "are interactive and used primarily to form or alter an ongoing process or activity. In contrast, assessments that come at the end of a process or activity, when it is difficult to alter or rectify what has already occurred, are called summative assessments" (pp.135–136).

Although the terms *formative* and *summative* have both been widely used in literature on classroom assessment, formative assessment has received more attention in the research literature. Specifically, formative classroom assessment has been the focus of almost every major attempt to synthesize the research on classroom assessment. Recall the finding from Black and Wiliam's (1998) synthesis of more than 250 studies that formative assessments, as opposed to summative ones, produce the more powerful effect on student learning. In his review of the research, Terrance Crooks (1988) reports that effect sizes for summative assessments are consistently lower than effect sizes for formative assessments. In short, it is formative assessment that has a strong research base supporting its impact on learning.

Unfortunately, within the research literature, formative assessment is not defined consistently. As Black and Wiliam (1998) note, "Formative assessment does not have a tightly defined and widely accepted meaning" (p. 7). For the purposes of this book, I use the definition offered by Black and Wiliam that formative assessment encompasses "all those activities undertaken by teachers and/or by students which provide information to be used as feedback to modify the teaching and learning activities in which they engage" (pp. 7–8). This definition casts a wide net in terms of both types of activities that qualify as assessments and the timing of those activities. By definition, then, formative classroom assessment can and should begin immediately within a learning episode and span its entire duration. Additionally, formative classroom assessment can take a wide variety of formats, both formal (e.g., paper-and-pencil quiz) and informal (e.g., a discussion with a student).

The Importance of Frequency

One of the strongest findings from the research is that the frequency of assessments is related to student academic achievement. This finding was dramatically demonstrated in the meta-analysis by Robert Bangert-Drowns, James Kulik, and Chen-Lin Kulik (1991). They analyzed findings from 29 studies on the frequency of assessments. Their findings are depicted in Figure 1.3.

To interpret the figure, assume that we are examining the learning of a particular student taking a 15-week course. (For a discussion of how this figure was constructed, see Technical Note 1.4.) The figure depicts the increase in learning

FIGURE 1.3
Gain Associated with Number of Assessments over 15 Weeks

Number of Assessments	Effect Size	Percentile-Point Gain
0	0	0
1	.34	13.5
5	.53	20.0
10	.60	22.5
15	.66	24.5
20	.71	26.0
25	.78	28.5
30	.80	29.0

Note: Effect sizes from data reported by Bangert-Drowns, Kulik, and Kulik (1991).

that one might expect when differing numbers of formative assessments are used during that 15-week session. If the teacher uses 5 assessments, a gain in student achievement of 20 percentile points is expected; if the teacher administers 25 assessments, a gain in student achievement of 28.5 percentile points is expected; and so on. Bangert-Drowns, Kulik, and Kulik (1991) comment on a number of aspects of this finding. First, they emphasize the relatively strong effect of a single assessment—13.5 percentile points, as depicted in Figure 1.3. Second, they highlight the fact that the frequency effect of assessment tapers off over time. As shown in Figure 1.3, the effect of assessment jumps dramatically from 0 to 10 assessments and then tends to level off. The recommendation from Bangert-Drowns, Kulik, and Kulik is not that teachers should use 30 assessments over a 15-week period but that teachers should systematically use classroom assessments as a form of feedback.

Fuchs and Fuchs (1986) reported this same phenomenon in their meta-analysis of 21 controlled studies. They reported that providing two assessments per week results in an effect size of .85, or a percentile gain of 30 points. Although there is no set number of assessments that should be administered during a unit of instruction or a grading period, the message from the research is clear: systematic use of classroom assessments—weekly or even more frequently—can have a strong positive effect on student achievement.

Summary and Conclusions

Research supports the conclusion that formative classroom assessment is one of the most powerful tools a classroom teacher might use. Formative assessments are defined as any activity that provides sound feedback on student learning. Characteristics of sound feedback include that it should be frequent, give students a clear picture of their progress and how they might improve, and provide encouragement. In the remaining chapters, these principles are used to design a comprehensive system of effective classroom assessment.

2

The Role of
State Standards

The first research-based generalization discussed in Chapter 1 attested to the need for assessment to provide a clear picture of student progress on learning goals. This chapter deals with the role state and national standards play in the articulation of clear learning goals.

It is no exaggeration to say that the standards movement has permeated K–12 education in the United States. Robert Glaser and Robert Linn (1993) explain:

> In the recounting of our nation's drive toward educational reform, the last decade of this century will undoubtedly be identified as the time when a concentrated press for national educational standards emerged. The press for standards was evidenced by the efforts of federal and state legislators, presidential and gubernatorial candidates, teachers and subject-matter specialists, councils, governmental agencies, and private foundations. (p. xiii)

Glaser and Linn made their comments at the end of the 20th century. There is no indication that the standards movement has lost any momentum at the beginning of the 21st century. Forty-nine states have developed standards (with Iowa being the lone exception) designed to guide what is to be taught in school. Also, one might make the case that even if the current standards movement faltered, the need to identify what students should know and be able to do in specific subject areas would survive, albeit under a different banner (for a discussion, see Lauer et al., 2005).

With regard to classroom assessment, one might infer that standards represent what should be assessed in schools. That is, given that the standards movement has identified what students should know and be able to do, and given the research cited in Chapter 1, properly executed classroom assessment of state standards should be at the top of every district's list of strategies to ensure that no child is left behind. Unfortunately, two barriers stand in the way of standards being the focus of effective classroom assessment: (1) too much content and (2) lack of unidimensionality.

Too Much Content

As powerful as the standards movement has been in the United States, it has probably generated as many problems as it has solutions. One of the most glaring is that standards documents articulate an inordinate amount of content. To illustrate, researchers at Mid-continent Research for Education and Learning (McREL) identified some 200 standards and 3,093 benchmarks in national- and state-level documents across 14 subject areas (Kendall & Marzano, 2000). The researchers then asked classroom teachers how long it would take to adequately address the content in those standards and benchmarks. When the researchers compared the amount of time it would take to teach the content in the standards with the amount of time that is available for classroom instruction, they found that 71 percent more instructional time than is now available would be required to address the mandated content in the standards documents (Marzano, Kendall, & Gaddy, 1999). Another way of looking at this is that schooling, as currently configured, would have to be extended from kindergarten to grade 21 or 22 to accommodate all the standards and benchmarks in the national documents. This is certainly not possible. Indeed, it is highly improbable that a school district will add even a few days to the school year. As Herbert Walberg (1997) has noted, the cost of adding even a few days to the academic year of a moderate-size district is prohibitive.

Even if time could be added to the school year, it would not be advisable to teach all the content found in the national and state standards documents. Although this might sound heretical at first, a comparison of U.S. standards with those of other countries leads to the inevitable conclusion that we have identified far too much content for our, or any other, K–12 education system. As reported in the Third International Mathematics and Science Survey, or TIMSS (Schmidt, McKnight, & Raizen, 1996), U.S. mathematics textbooks attempt to cover 175 percent as many topics as do German textbooks and 350 percent as many topics as do Japanese textbooks. Similarly, U.S. science textbooks attempt to cover more than nine times as many topics as do German textbooks and more than four times as many topics as do Japanese textbooks. Yet, in spite of their exposure to far fewer topics, German and Japanese students significantly outperform U.S. students in mathematics and science. This makes intuitive sense upon close scrutiny. If the curriculum presents more topics than time allows, those topics are addressed at a superficial level only.

What is a district or school to do? The straightforward but not simple answer is to dramatically decrease the amount of content teachers are expected to address in class. To do so, a school or district must distinguish between the content that is essential for all students to learn versus that which is not. Many curriculum researchers and theorists have presented this concept. For example, Fenwick English (2000) recommends that schools conduct an audit to determine the amount of time necessary to teach the content identified in the curriculum. When a school determines that there is more content than can be adequately addressed in the time available, the content must be trimmed to fit within the time parameters. Douglas Reeves (2002) and Larry Ainsworth (2003a, 2003b) have forwarded the concept of "unpacking" standards documents, identifying what is essential, and organizing the essential content into a small set of "power standards." In their book *Understanding by Design* (2005), Grant Wiggins and Jay McTighe have also promoted the idea of recasting state standards in the form of overarching, or enduring understandings. These are noteworthy recommendations, but they represent time-consuming, technical tasks. In this chapter, I present my own version of the sequence of activities recommended by Reeves, Ainsworth, Wiggins, McTighe, and others.

Lack of Unidimensionality

Even after it has been trimmed to fit within the time available for instruction, the essential content found in standards documents must be reorganized and restated to make it amenable to formative classroom assessment. This requirement results from a basic principle underlying measurement theory—the principle of unidimensionality. In simple terms, *unidimensionality* means that a single score on a test represents a single dimension or trait that has been assessed. This concept underpins almost all of measurement theory within education and psychology. To illustrate, in a foundational article on measurement theory, Frederick Lord (1959) explains that a test "is a collection of tasks; the examinee's performance on these tasks is taken as an index of his standing along some psychological dimension." In effect, Lord's comments imply that any test that depicts a student's performance on the test by a single score should, by definition, measure one trait only. Interestingly, classroom assessments, standardized assessments, and state assessments frequently violate this assumption. Indeed, researcher John Hattie (1984, 1985; Hattie, Krakowski, Rogers, & Swaminathan, 1996) has chronicled how difficult it is to design a unidimensional test and how frequently the assumption of unidimensionality is violated (see Technical Note 2.1).

To demonstrate the consequences of violating the unidimensionality assumption, consider a test with 20 items. Ten of the items measure a specific trait or dimension, such as an understanding of different types of genre in literature. We call this Dimension A. The other 10 items on the test measure a second dimension unrelated to Dimension A, such as the ability to edit for grammar. We call this Dimension B. Next, consider the scores for three students on this 20-item test:

	Dimension A	Dimension B	Total Score
Student 1	2	10	12
Student 2	10	2	12
Student 3	6	6	12

All three students received the same total score, 12. Yet their profiles were quite different across the two dimensions. Student 1 performed well on Dimension B but poorly on Dimension A. Student 2 exhibited the opposite pattern, performing well on A but not B. Student 3 demonstrated the same performance on A and B, which might be described as "fair" in terms of knowledge. We return to the concept of unidimensionality in later chapters when we consider how to score classroom assessments. There we will see that placing a single total score on a test with two or more dimensions makes little sense. Rather, the principle of unidimensionality tells us that a score for each dimension should be provided.

In terms of state and national standards documents, the principle of unidimensionality implies that the various knowledge dimensions or traits within the standards should be clearly delineated. Unfortunately, this is rarely the case. To illustrate, consider the following benchmark statement from the mathematics standards document published by the National Council of Teachers of Mathematics (NCTM), which articulates what students should know and be able to do by the end of 5th grade:

• Develop fluency in adding, subtracting, multiplying, and dividing whole numbers. (NCTM, 2000, p. 392)

The information and skill in the benchmark are certainly related in that they all involve computation of whole numbers. However, the underlying processes are not the same and, in fact, might be quite different. This conclusion has been dramatically illustrated by cognitive psychologists who have identified the actual steps in cognitive processes such as addition, subtraction, multiplication, and division (see Anderson, 1983). This single benchmark probably addresses four separate dimensions:

- The process of adding whole numbers
- The process of subtracting whole numbers
- The process of multiplying whole numbers
- The process of dividing whole numbers

This example is informative in itself because it demonstrates how much subject matter content might be embedded in standards documents. Specifically, the NCTM standards document contains only 241 benchmarks that span kindergarten through grade 12. One might assume that the NCTM document thus addresses 241 dimensions. However, when I "unpacked" the NCTM benchmark statements in a procedure like that demonstrated here, I found 741 unique elements (Marzano, 2002b). A review of other standards documents reveals that the NCTM materials are typical.

Standards documents, then, as currently written provide teachers with little guidance as to the dimensions they address. Without such guidance, standards documents are difficult to use as the basis for a well-articulated system of formative classroom assessment.

Overcoming the Barriers

As formidable as the barriers might seem, they can be overcome if a district or school is willing to reconstitute the knowledge in their standards documents. This need to reconstitute state standards and benchmarks has been addressed by many researchers, theorists, and consultants who work with districts and schools to implement standards-based education (see Ainsworth, 2003a, 2003b; Reeves, 2002; Wiggins & McTighe, 2005). Precisely how to reconstitute standards documents is not quite as clear-cut as the need to do so. In science, the American Association for the Advancement of Science (2001) has recommended that the national science standards be reorganized into "clusters," such as the structure of matter, cells, flow of matter and energy, and evolution of life. Reeves and Ainsworth promote the construction of "power standards." Wiggins and McTighe promote the notion of overarching or enduring understandings. John Kendall (2000) has proposed that standards and benchmarks be reconstituted as "topics." He explains:

> Forty-nine states have published standards for K–12 education. Most of the state documents organize content in a similar format, and the standard documents issued by districts and schools often follow suit. This organization is fairly straightforward. The topmost and broadest level, usually called the *standard*, is a category that helps to slice a subject area into manageable chunks. The labels for these categories range from single words to lengthy sentences, but they serve the same purpose. In mathematics, for

example, labels can usually be found that denote areas such as measurement, computation, and geometry, among others. The finest or lowest level of organization is the heart of standards, called, variously, the *benchmark*, the *objective*, or the *indicator*. This level of organization describes what students should know and be able to do. (p. 37)

Yet Kendall cautions that these two levels—the very broad level of the standard and the very specific level of the benchmark, objective, or indicator—do not serve well as practical tools for educators. He proposes an "interim" structure, referred to as a *topic*. According to Kendall, a topic can be defined as "somewhere between the breadth of a standard and the specificity of a benchmark" (p. 38). He further explains that a *topic* has three basic purposes:

• Providing teachers with an easier way to find appropriate information for instruction

• Making clearer the connections between benchmarks within and across the subject areas

• Providing a useful level of specificity for feedback to students

Kendall's topics are focused on instruction. I have found that for the purpose of classroom assessment, it is more useful to use the term *measurement topic*, defined loosely as categories of highly related dimensions. I recommend three steps for the design of measurement topics.

Step 1: Unpack the Benchmarks in Standards Documents

The first step in designing effective measurement topics is to "unpack" the benchmarks in standards documents, as demonstrated in the example involving the NCTM benchmark statement. A technical protocol for unpacking benchmarks is described in Marzano (2002b). Briefly, though, it is a simple matter of identifying the unique elements of information and skill in each benchmark statement. I have found that subject matter specialists are quite skilled and efficient at doing this. Consequently, a district need only assemble its expert mathematics teachers and curriculum specialist to unpack the mathematics standards, assemble the expert science teachers and curriculum specialist to unpack the science standards, and so on.

To illustrate again, this time using content areas other than mathematics, consider the following science benchmark, intended for grades K through 4, from the *National Science Education Standards* (National Research Council, 1996):

• Light travels in a straight line until it strikes an object. Light can be reflected by a mirror, refracted by a lens, or absorbed by the object.

> • Heat can be produced in many ways, such as burning, rubbing, or mixing one substance with another. Heat can move from one object to another by conduction.
> • Electricity in circuits can produce light, heat, sound, and magnetic effects.
> • Electrical circuits require a complete loop through which an electrical current can pass.
> • Magnets attract and repel each other and certain kinds of other materials. (p. 127)

This benchmark addresses at least five dimensions, one for each of the bullets. The science example presented here, and the mathematics example before it, are from national standards documents. State standards documents exhibit the same problem (multiple dimensions) in their benchmark statements.

To illustrate, consider the following 5th grade benchmark for the "measurement" standard from the Ohio state standards document entitled *Academic Content Standards: K–12 Mathematics* (Ohio Department of Education, 2001):

1. Identify and select appropriate units to measure angles; i.e., degrees.
2. Identify paths between points on a grid or coordinate plane and compare the lengths of the paths; e.g., shortest path, paths of equal length.
3. Demonstrate and describe the differences between covering the faces (surface area) and filling the interior (volume) of three-dimensional objects.
4. Demonstrate understanding of the differences among linear units, square units, and cubic units.
5. Make conversions within the same measurement system while performing computations.
6. Use strategies to develop formulas for determining perimeter and area of triangles, rectangles, and parallelograms, and volume of rectangular prisms.
7. Use benchmark angles (e.g., 45°, 90°, 120°) to estimate the measure of angles, and use a tool to measure and draw angles. (pp. 72–73)

Again, this single benchmark includes many dimensions—by design at least seven and probably more if one unpacks each statement. For example, the sixth statement addresses developing formulas for perimeter; area of triangles, rectangles, and parallelograms; and volume of rectangular prisms. Each of these might represent a single dimension in that a student could be competent in one but not in the others.

The examples of the national standards for mathematics and science and the state mathematics standards from Ohio are not intended as a criticism of these specific documents. Virtually any national or state document for any subject area could have been used with the same outcome. National and state standards documents simply were not designed to allow for easy application to classroom assessments. All documents must be "unpacked" to identify their specific knowledge dimensions.

Step 2: Identify the Dimensions That Are Essential for All Students to Learn

When standards benchmark statements have been unpacked, a district or school is likely to find far more content than they originally imagined. Recall that when I unpacked the 241 benchmark statements from the NCTM standards document, I found 741 dimensions. This massive array of content must be pared substantially to fit into the time available for instruction. Again, expert teachers and curriculum specialists can do this efficiently.

To illustrate, consider the aforementioned study I conducted using mathematics dimensions (Marzano, 2002b). Specifically, 10 mathematics educators were presented with 741 mathematics dimensions drawn from the national mathematics standards (National Council of Teachers of Mathematics, 2000) and asked to identify those that were essential for all students to learn regardless of their future aspirations. Each educator independently rated each of the 741 dimensions relatively quickly. Combining the ratings produced a list of 404 essential dimensions. In other words, the initial list was reduced by 46 percent (see Marzano, 2002b). Following this same basic process, to overcome the barrier of too much content, a district or school need only convene its subject matter specialists and task them with identifying the content necessary for all students to learn.

After expert teachers and curriculum specialists have made the first cut at determining essential content, the district may choose to involve the community at large. To illustrate, in the early 1990s consultants from McREL worked with a local school district to identify the essential content all students in the district were expected to master. The initial list of essential elements was published in the local newspaper in a special supplement. (To communicate clearly with the community, the district used the term *essential elements* as opposed to *dimensions* or *traits*.) Each essential element was accompanied by a question asking community members if they thought the knowledge statement represented content that was truly essential for all students to learn. Community members who filled out the supplement sent their responses to the district office. These responses were tabulated, and a percentage score representing the level of agreement by community members was computed for each statement. The subject matter experts from the district then used the responses from community members to revise the essential elements where appropriate. In the final analysis, educators and community members alike considered the essential elements to be representative of their values regarding the education of the district's K–12 students. (For more discussion, see Marzano & Kendall, 1996.)

Step 3: Organize the Dimensions into Categories
of Related Information and Skills

The third step in the design of measurement topics is to organize the dimensions identified as essential into categories of related elements. Of course, the critical aspect of this step is clarity about the meaning of the term *related*. This issue is clarified nicely by the concept of *covariance*.

Covariance is discussed more rigorously in Technical Note 2.2. Briefly, though, *covariance* means that as ability in one dimension increases, so does that in another (Shadish, Cook, & Campbell, 2002). Covariance of dimensions is partly a function of instruction. To illustrate, reconsider the dimensions that were embedded in the NCTM benchmark discussed earlier:

- The process of adding whole numbers
- The process of subtracting whole numbers
- The process of multiplying whole numbers
- The process of dividing whole numbers

A case can be made that these dimensions are somewhat independent in that a student might be fairly proficient at adding whole numbers but not proficient at subtracting whole numbers. On the other hand, a case can be made that addition and subtraction of whole numbers have overlapping steps and, perhaps more important, are typically taught in tandem. The fact that they overlap and are taught together implies that they covary. As skill in one dimension goes up, so does skill in the other. Thus, "related" dimensions that would be combined to form a measurement topic overlap in their component parts and are commonly taught together or are taught in relationship to one another.

To get a sense of a measurement topic composed of covarying dimensions, consider Figure 2.1, which lists the covarying dimensions for a measurement topic entitled *Reading for Main Idea*. (Note that Figure 2.1 does not represent the final format for a measurement topic. Chapter 3 presents a "rubric-based" format in which measurement topics should be articulated.) At grades 9 and 10, the measurement topic states that while reading grade-appropriate material, the student identifies and articulates the major patterns of ideas in the text such as the following:

- Complex causal relationships
- Arguments with complex systems of support
- Problems with complex solutions
- Complex plots with multiple story lines

FIGURE 2.1
Covarying Dimensions for the Measurement Topic *Reading for Main Idea*

Stem	While reading grade-appropriate material, the student identifies and articulates the major patterns of ideas in the text, such as
Grade 9 (Lower Division)	• Complex causal relationships • Arguments with complex systems of support • Problems with complex solutions • Complex plots with multiple story lines
Grade 8	• Complex causal relationships • Basic arguments • Problems with complex solutions • Complex plots with multiple story lines
Grade 7	• Complex causal relationships • Basic arguments • Problems with complex solutions • Plots with single story lines
Grade 6	• Complex causal relationships • Basic arguments • Complex chronologies • Problems with basic solutions • Plots with single story lines
Grade 5	• Complex causal relationships • Complex chronologies • Problems with basic solutions • Plots with single story lines
Grade 4	• Basic cause and effect • Simple chronologies • Problems with basic solutions • Plots with single story lines
Grade 3	• Basic cause and effect • Simple chronologies • Problems with basic solutions • Plots with single story lines
Grade 2	• Basic cause and effect • Plots with single story lines
Grade 1	• Plots with simple story lines
Grade K	Not applicable

At the heart of this measurement topic is the ability to identify patterns of information in texts. One might say that this dynamic operationally defines *reading for the main idea*. For example, if a student reads the book *The Red Badge of Courage*, an important part of understanding the main idea of the book is identifying the various aspects of the plot and discerning the various story lines (i.e., *identifying complex plots with multiple story lines*). If a student reads an editorial on the benefits of strictly enforced environmental laws, understanding the main idea of the editorial is synonymous with discerning the basic aspects of the implicit and explicit arguments laid out by the author (i.e., *identifying arguments with complex systems of support*).

To include these dimensions in the same measurement topic is to assert that as students' ability to identify patterns of information involving complex plots with multiple story lines increases, so too does their ability to identify patterns of information involving complex arguments—as does their ability to identify patterns of information involving complex causal relationships, and so on.

As we shall see in Chapter 3, articulating measurement topics as shown in Figure 2.1 makes it relatively easy to develop formative classroom assessments. It also clearly delineates what teachers are to address from one grade level to the next. Consider the progression of covarying elements from grade 1 through grades 9 and 10. Four elements are listed for grades 9 and 10. At grade 8, four elements are also listed. Some elements are the same. For example, both levels involve the dimensions of identifying complex plots with multiple story lines and identifying problems with complex solutions. However, at grades 9 and 10 students are expected to recognize arguments with complex systems of support, whereas at grade 8 they are expected to recognize basic arguments.

From one grade level to another, then, the covarying dimensions within a measurement topic become more sophisticated and more complex. Additionally, some dimensions might end at a particular grade level. For example, the dimension of identifying chronologies ends at grade 6. This indicates that in the district's curricular scheme, chronologies are addressed in grades 3 through 6, beginning with simple chronologies in grade 3 and ending with complex chronologies in grade 6. In summary, measurement topics should reflect the instructional values and practices of a school district.

Guidelines for Designing a Comprehensive System of Measurement Topics

As the preceding discussion illustrates, designing a comprehensive system of measurement topics is a complex endeavor. However, as later chapters of this book demonstrate, a well-articulated system of topics is a necessary prerequisite for using classroom assessments to track student progress. Marzano and Haystead (in press) provide sample measurement topics for language arts, mathematics, science, and social studies. Additionally, the following recommendations will help districts design effective systems of measurement topics.

Limit Measurement Topics to 20 or Fewer per Subject Area and Grade Level

Given that one of the main barriers to implementing standards is that they contain too much content, it would be counterproductive to identify too many measurement topics. I recommend no more than 20 measurement topics per subject, per grade level, and ideally about 15.

To illustrate, Figure 2.2 provides a list of possible measurement topics for language arts, mathematics, science, and social studies. It is important to note that the list in Figure 2.2 is a sample only. Districts must articulate their own topics, reflecting the content in their state standards and the priorities of their teachers and the community. In working with a number of districts, I have found that they are quite diverse in what they name their measurement topics but quite similar in the dimensions they identify to populate those measurement topics.

Notice that 12 topics are listed for language arts, 18 for mathematics, 13 for science, and 13 for social studies. The figure does not show grade spans. In practice, all measurement topics do not span all grade levels. For example, the measurement topics in mathematics of *addition/subtraction* and *multiplication/division* begin in kindergarten and end at grade 5. The measurement topics *ratio/proportion/ percent* and *graphing coordinate planes* don't start until grade 6. In effect, then, even though mathematics has 18 measurement topics, any particular grade level has fewer than 18. Also note that the topics are grouped under categories. Districts and schools use different terms to refer to these categories, such as *strands, themes,* and even *standards.*

If the number of topics is few enough at a particular grade level, some topics can be addressed repeatedly within a given year. Some topics might be addressed during one quarter only, whereas others might be addressed every quarter. For example, in 3rd grade, mathematics measurement topics *addition/subtraction* and *multiplication/division* might be addressed each quarter, whereas the topic *lines/angles/figures* might be addressed in one quarter only.

A well-articulated set of measurement topics goes a long way toward implementing what I have referred to elsewhere as "a guaranteed and viable curriculum" (Marzano, 2003). This concept is described in depth in the book *What Works in Schools.* Briefly, however, a district that has such a curriculum can guarantee that

FIGURE 2.2
Sample Measurement Topics

Language Arts

Reading
1. Word recognition and vocabulary
2. Reading for main idea
3. Literary analysis

Writing
4. Language conventions
5. Organization and focus
6. Research and technology
7. Evaluation and revision
8. Writing applications

Listening and Speaking
9. Comprehension
10. Organization and delivery
11. Analysis and evaluation of oral media
12. Speaking applications

Mathematics

Number Sense
1. Number systems
2. Operational relationships
3. Estimation

Computation
4. Addition/subtraction
5. Multiplication/division
6. Operations
7. Ratio/proportion/percent

Algebra and Functions
8. Algebraic concepts
9. Graphing coordinate planes

Geometry
10. Lines/angles, figures
11. Motion geometry

Measurement
12. Practical applications
13. Dimensional measurement

Data Analysis/Probability
14. Visual representation
15. Statistics
16. Probability

Problem Solving
17. Strategies/reasoning
18. Validity of results

Science

The Nature of Science
1. History of science
2. The scientific method
3. Technology

Application of Science
4. Mathematics and the language of science
5. Communication in science
6. Common themes

Physical Science
7. Matter and energy
8. Forces of nature
9. Diversity of life
10. Human identity
11. Interdependence of life

Earth Science
12. The Earth and the processes that shape it
13. The universe

Social Studies

Citizenship/Government/Democracy
1. Rights, responsibilities, and participation in the political process
2. The U.S. and state constitutions
3. The civil and criminal legal systems

Culture and Cultural Diversity
4. The influence of culture
5. Similarities and differences within and between cultures

Production, Distribution, and Consumption
6. The nature and function of economic systems
7. Economics at the local, state, national, and global levels
8. Personal economics

Time, Continuity, and Change
9. Individuals and events that have shaped history
10. Current events and the modern world
11. Influence of the past, present, and future

People, Places, and Environments
12. Spatial thinking and the use of charts, maps, and graphs
13. The impact of geography on people and events

no matter who teaches a given course or grade level, certain topics will be adequately addressed. Obviously, teachers must keep track of specific measurement topics to fulfill this requirement. For such a guarantee to be valid, the district must have few enough measurement topics to ensure that the process of keeping track of the topics is viable—teachers can do so in the time available to them.

Include Measurement Topics for Life Skills

A number of studies and reports over the last few decades have noted the importance of "life skills"—information and skills that are not specific to traditional academic subject areas but are important to success in a variety of situations. For example, the 1991 report by the Secretary's Commission on Achieving Necessary Skills (SCANS) entitled *What Work Requires of Schools: A SCANS Report for America 2000* notes that the authors spent 12 months "talking to business owners, to public employees, to the people who manage employees daily, to union officials, and to workers on the line and at their desks. We have talked to them in their stores, shops, government offices, and manufacturing facilities" (p. v). This extensive study generated a comprehensive list of critical work skills, or life skills. It included behaviors such as effort, working well in groups, adhering to company policies, problem solving, and thinking and reasoning.

A complementary work to the SCANS report, *Workplace Basics: The Essential Skills Employers Want* (Carnevale, Gainer, & Meltzer, 1990), was sponsored by the American Society for Training and Development (ASTD). The report summarized the opinions of "approximately 50,000 practitioners, managers, administrators, educators, and researchers in the field of human resource development" (p. xiii). Again, the report attested to the importance of things such as punctuality, respect, and an honest day's work.

The SCANS report and *Workplace Basics* focused on employers. Studies that have polled parents and guardians have reported similar findings. For example, the report *First Things First: What Americans Expect from Public Schools* (Farkas, Friedman, Boese, & Shaw, 1994), sponsored by the polling firm Public Agenda, noted that 88 percent of those surveyed said that schools should teach work-related competencies such as self-discipline, punctuality, and dependability. In a general survey of adults in the United States conducted by the Gallup Corporation under the direction of McREL researchers, respondents rated life skills higher than 13 academic subject areas such as mathematics, science, history, language arts, and physical education as definitely required for all students to learn before high school graduation (Marzano, Kendall, & Cicchinelli, 1998). Finally, the Partnership for 21st Century Skills (www.21stcenturyskills.org) has determined that life skills are so important to success in the new century that they should be heavily emphasized in K–12 education.

Given the importance of these life skills and the apparently strong mandate from the world of work to teach and reinforce them in schools, I recommend that measurement topics should be designed to address them. The following are life skill topics commonly identified as important by districts:

• **Participation** refers to the extent to which students make an effort to be engaged in class and respond to the tasks presented to them.

• **Work completion** involves the extent to which students adhere to the requirements regarding the tasks assigned to them. It involves students turning in assignments in a timely fashion and following the conventions that the teacher has established (e.g., format considerations for a report).

• **Behavior** involves the extent to which students adhere to the rules for conduct and behavior. This includes rules set by individual teachers and those established schoolwide.

• **Working in groups** addresses the extent to which students actively participate in the accomplishment of group goals. This category does not include student behavior within a group, which is addressed by the category *behavior*. Rather, it is focused on the extent to which students participate in the accomplishment of group goals as opposed to focusing only on their own goals.

As with academic measurement topics, covarying dimensions should be articulated for each life skill measurement topic at each grade level. However, the life skill measurement topics will probably have more overlap of dimensions from one grade level to the next. To illustrate, a district might identify the following dimensions or elements for the life skill topic *participation*:

• Making an attempt to answer questions asked by the teacher
• Volunteering ideas without being called on
• Paying attention to presentations

Instead of listing different dimensions for each grade level, these might be identified as important to all middle school grade levels.

Change the Structure of Measurement Topics at the High School Level

The approach to measurement topics described thus far works well for kindergarten through grade 8 and even into the first two years of high school—grades 9 and 10. That is, it makes sense to have measurement topics that become progressively more complex in terms of the covarying elements from grade level to grade level. However, this approach does not work well in the course structure used by most high schools, because high school courses tend to be more diverse in the content they address. For example, high schools will typically offer courses such as Algebra I, Algebra II, Geometry, Trigonometry, and so on, whereas elementary schools will offer *mathematics*. One solution is to think in terms of "lower-division" and "upper-division" courses in high school.

The distinction between lower- and upper-division courses has been characteristic of discussions on high school reform for some time, although different terminology has been used. For example, the notion of the Certificate of Initial Mastery (CIM) and the Certificate of Advanced Mastery (CAM) was first proposed by the Commission on the Skills of the American Work Force in its 1990 report entitled *America's Choice: High Skills or Low Wages* (in Rothman, 1995). In general, the CIM represents expectations of what a 16-year-old student should know and be able to do. This expectation is similar to what some have referred to as "general literacy standards"—the information and skills that are required to function well within the general population. (For a discussion, see Marzano & Kendall, 1996.) In contrast, the CAM represents expectations for students who seek postsecondary study in a given subject area. This notion is similar to what has been referred to by some as "advanced standards" or "world-class standards." For example, Goal 4 of the six goals set at the first education summit in September 1989 in Charlottesville, Virginia, explicitly referred to the need for world-class standards in U.S. schools:

> Goal 4: By the year 2000, U.S. students will be first in the world in science and mathematics achievement. (National Education Goals Panel, 1991, p. 4)

The need for advanced standards that raise the performance of students in the United States to a level that matches or exceeds those of other countries was reinforced at the second education summit in March 1996 at Palisades, New York: "As Governors, we commit to the development and establishment of internationally competitive academic standards" (National Governors Association, 1996, p. 4).

Operationally, the distinction between advanced standards and basic or literacy standards and the distinction between the CIM and the CAM imply that for introductory high school courses, a school or district would use the same measurement topics that have been articulated for kindergarten through 8th grade. This is why Figure 2.2 lists covarying elements from kindergarten through grade 10. The logic here is that the covarying elements listed for grades 9 and 10 address the dimensions that would be the focus of lower-division courses in language arts. For upper-division or advanced courses, entirely new measurement topics would be articulated, reflecting the more advanced content in those courses.

Allow for a Teacher-Choice Measurement Topic

The final suggestion I typically make to districts and schools is to allow for a "teacher-choice" measurement topic for every subject area at every grade level. If a district or school has been truly efficient in designing its measurement topics, there should be room for this option. As its name implies, a teacher-choice topic involves content considered important by a teacher but not reflected in the measurement topics articulated by the district or school. In effect, this option allows teachers to supplement the district or school curriculum in a way that recognizes the unique set of experiences and background they bring to the subject matter. For example, a 10th grade English teacher might have an extensive background in journalism, but the district or school has nothing in its measurement topics that reflect journalism skills such as these:

- Being objective when reporting on an incident
- Keeping the focus on the story not the reporter
- Validating eyewitness accounts

It makes sense that a district or school might want to provide enough flexibility in its system of measurement topics to accommodate the individual strengths of teachers it has hired.

Summary and Conclusions

Districts and schools need to reconstitute the knowledge in state standards in the form of measurement topics. To do so, they may use a three-step process that involves unpacking the standards, identifying the dimensions that are essential for all students to learn, and organizing the dimensions into categories of related information and skills. Following various recommendations will ensure that a system of measurement topics is flexible enough to fit well in a comprehensive K–12 system. Without reconstituting state standards documents, there is little chance that teachers can use them effectively as the basis for formative classroom assessment.

3

A Scale That Measures
Learning over Time

One of the four generalizations from the research literature presented in Chapter 1 was that classroom assessments should be formative in nature, and by definition formative assessments measure growth in learning. How, then, does a teacher assess in a way that measures growth in learning? This chapter examines that issue. We begin by taking a critical look at the point system, which is the assessment system that many teachers use.

Why the Point System Falls Short

At first, asking "How does a teacher assess in a way that measures growth in learning?" might seem like a non sequitur. One might assume that all a teacher needs to do is administer a series of assessments for a given measurement topic over a grading period and examine the pattern of scores over time. For example, if a teacher wished to track student growth in learning for a specific science measurement topic over a quarter, she would construct a number of assessments that address the topic. In all, she might administer four tests of the topic—a pretest at the beginning of the quarter, two tests at the end of the third week and the sixth week, respectively, and an end-of-quarter post-test. If the teacher scored all the tests using a 100-point, or percentage, scale, tracking student learning would be a simple matter of examining the upward progression of scores for each student across the four assessments. A pattern of scores like the following would indicate that a student had learned quite a bit: 56, 60, 75, and 86. However, a pattern of scores like the following would indicate that the student did not learn a great deal: 65, 68, 70, and 71.

As intuitively appealing as this system might appear, it has one major flaw—the scores on the various tests are typically not comparable in terms of students' understanding and skill regarding a specific measurement topic. That is, just because a student receives a score of 56 on the first test and 60 on the second test doesn't necessarily mean she has increased her understanding and skill by 4 percentage points. In fact, research indicates that the score a student receives on a test is more dependent on who scores the test and how they score it than it is on what the student knows and understands. To illustrate, consider a study that examined an 8th grade science test (see Marzano, 2002a) with six constructed-response items—items that required students to explain their answers as opposed to selecting among multiple-choice items.

Ten students took the test, and their responses were scored independently by five teachers, all of whom were experienced 8th grade science teachers familiar with the content on the test. However, before scoring the 10 students' responses, each teacher carefully read the test items and assigned points to the items based on the perceived importance of the content addressed in each item. This, of course, is a common practice recommended in many texts on classroom assessment (see Airasian, 1994; Brookhart, 2004; McMillan, 2000).

Although this practice seems perfectly reasonable, it creates havoc in terms of interpreting and comparing students' scores simply because different teachers will assign different weights to items. To illustrate, consider Figure 3.1, which shows the points assigned by each teacher to each item. Immediately below each point designation is the percentage of the total represented by the points. For example, Teacher 1 assigned a total of 50 points across the six items, with 10 points going to items 1 and 3; 15 points to item 2; and 5 points each to items 4, 5, and 6. The items assigned 10 points each account for 20 percent of the total score, the item assigned 15 points accounts for 30 percent of the total score, and the items worth 5 points each account for 10 percent of the total.

The item weights assigned by the teachers show a definite pattern. All teachers assigned items 1, 2, and 3 more points than items 4, 5, and 6. However, the teachers were not consistent in the number of points they assigned. The most discrepant pattern of weighting was that of Teacher 3, who assigned 45 points to the first item and 15 points to items 2 and 3. As computed by Teacher 3, then, the relative contribution of these three items to the total score a student might receive was 50 percent, 16.7 percent, and 16.7 percent, respectively. In contrast, the relative contribution of the first three items for Teacher 1 was 20 percent, 30 percent, and 20 percent.

FIGURE 3.1
Five Teachers' Point Assignments by Items

Teacher		Item 1	2	3	4	5	6	Total
1	Pts.	10	15	10	5	5	5	50
	%	20.0	30.0	20.0	10.0	10.0	10.0	
2	Pts.	25	25	25	5	5	5	90
	%	27.8	27.8	27.8	5.6	5.6	5.6	
3	Pts.	45	15	15	5	5	5	90
	%	50.0	16.7	16.7	5.6	5.6	5.6	
4	Pts.	20	15	15	10	10	10	80
	%	25.0	18.8	18.8	12.5	12.5	12.5	
5	Pts.	20	20	20	10	10	10	90
	%	22.2	22.2	22.2	11.1	11.1	11.1	

Source: Marzano (2002a). Reprinted with permission.

The differences in the points or weights assigned to the items explain in part the wide variation in the students' final test scores. To illustrate, consider Figure 3.2 (p. 32), which reports each student's total score as computed by each teacher. When examining the figure, it is important to note that the total score for each student has been translated to a percentage, or 100-point, scale. To dramatize the differences in final scores for individual students from teacher to teacher, consider the total score for Student 2 as computed by Teacher 2 (91) versus Teacher 3 (50). This 41-point differential is the largest between teachers in the study, and it makes sense given the difference in their weighting schemes. Reexamining Figure 3.1, we see that Student 2 received a final percentage score of 91 from Teacher 2 because the student obtained the following points on the six items for a total of 82 points:

- 20 of 25 points for item 1
- 25 of 25 points for items 2 and 3
- 4 of 5 points for items 4, 5, and 6

Getting 82 out of 90 points translates to a percentage score of 91.

Student 2 received a final percentage score of 50 percent from Teacher 3 based on the following point assignments:

FIGURE 3.2
Five Teachers' Total Scores for 10 Students on a 100-Point Scale

Student	Teacher				
	1	2	3	4	5
1	65	75	80	50	60
2	78	91	50	86	74
3	90	70	82	100	85
4	65	70	50	70	60
5	82	92	72	72	100
6	71	61	82	75	60
7	87	100	85	81	72
8	76	86	70	50	60
9	73	84	72	62	75
10	80	92	100	80	76

Source: Marzano (2002a). Reprinted with permission.

- 20 of 45 points for item 1
- 10 of 15 points for items 2 and 3
- 2 of 5 points for items 4 and 5
- 1 of 5 points for item 6

Getting 45 out of 90 points translates to a percentage score of 50.

This illustration also demonstrates another source of variation in teacher judgments inherent in the point system—differences in teachers' perceptions of the extent to which students' responses meet the ideal response. That is, when scoring a student's response for a given item, the teacher has in mind the type of response that would indicate total understanding or demonstration of a skill. If the student's response to an item matches this ideal, the student is assigned complete credit— the maximum number of points—for the item. If the student's response does not match the ideal, then the teacher develops some tacit system for assigning partial credit. A response that is three-fourths of the ideal receives 75 percent of the points for the item, a response that is half the ideal receives 50 percent of the points, and so on. As explained by Jeffrey Smith, Lisa Smith, and Richard DeLisi (2001), a teacher might typically "start with full credit for the correct answer, then deduct points as students move away from that correct answer" (p. 52).

FIGURE 3.3
How Teachers 2 and 3 Scored Student 2

	Item						Total Points	Student's Percentage Score
	1	2	3	4	5	6		
Teacher 2								
How many points item was worth	25	25	25	5	5	5	90	
How many points student's response was assigned	20	25	25	4	4	4	82	91%
Percentage of item answered correctly	80%	100%	100%	80%	80%	80%		
Teacher 3								
How many points item was worth	45	15	15	5	5	5	90	
How many points student's response was assigned	20	10	10	2	2	1	45	50%
Percentage of item answered correctly	44%	67%	67%	40%	40%	20%		

When scoring the science test used in this study, teachers disagreed on the extent to which students' responses to items met the ideal. To illustrate, let's look more closely at the specifics of how Teacher 2 and Teacher 3 scored each item for Student 2 (see Figure 3.3). Teacher 2 assigned Student 2 the following percentages of total possible credit for the six items: 80 percent of total credit for item 1; 100 percent of total credit for items 2 and 3; and 80 percent for items 4, 5, and 6. The student thus received 20 of 25 points for item 1; 25 of 25 points for items 2 and 3; and 4 of 5 points each for items 4, 5, and 6. The student's total points were 82 of 90, or 91 percent. In contrast, Teacher 3 assigned Student 2 the following percentages of total credit for the six items: 44 percent of total credit for item 1; 67 percent for items 2 and 3; 40 percent for items 4 and 5; and 20 percent for item 6. The student thus received 20 of 45 points for item 1; 10 of 15 points for items 2 and 3; 2 of 5 points for items 4 and 5; and 1 of 5 points for item 6. The student's 45 total points divided by 90 translates to 50 percent. In effect, the differences in the teachers' perceptions about how well the student answered the items were then multiplied by the differential weights or points the teachers had assigned to each item to exacerbate the differences in total score. Clearly, teachers may differ in many ways when they score assessments using the point system; the scores for students derived from the point system are not comparable from teacher to teacher.

Origins of the Point System

Given that the point system is the method of choice for scoring classroom assessments in spite of its inherent weaknesses, it is instructive to consider its origins. Measurement expert Darrel Bock (1997) traces the point system to World War I, when the U.S. Army designed and administered the Alpha Test to quickly and efficiently identify the competencies of hundreds of thousands of recruits. The test's purpose was to assess the aptitude of the new soldiers to place them in work roles most appropriate to their abilities. The test required a quick and efficient scoring system that could be applied to the multiple-choice items that were scored as correct or incorrect. Correct items were assigned one point; incorrect items were assigned no points. The summary score on a test was easily computed by forming the ratio of the number of correct items divided by the total number of items and multiplying by 100—the percentage score. Generally speaking, the Alpha Test was considered quite successful in that tens of thousands of recruits were assessed and scored quickly and efficiently. The success of the easily scored Alpha Test popularized the multiple-choice item and the percentage method of obtaining a summary score.

The multiple-choice format and a summary score based on the proportion of correct responses received a strong endorsement in the 1940s, when the College Entrance Examination Board (CEEB) commissioned psychologist Carl Bingham to develop the Scholastic Aptitude Test (SAT). The SAT was intended to predict success in college. Because of the ease of scoring multiple-choice items, the written portion of the examination was dropped by 1942. Before then, the written portion of the test was the most heavily weighted. By 1947 the multiple-choice format was a permanent fixture due in no small part to the development of mark-sense answer sheets that could be scored by machine. As Bock (1997) explains:

> Because the early equipment could do no more than count the number of pencil marks in correct boxes of the item alternatives, the number-correct score became by default the source datum for theoretical work in educational measurement. It became the main focus of test theory. (p. 23)

The perceived utility of the multiple-choice format and the percent-correct summary score soon spilled over into any item that could be scored as 1 or 0—

correct or incorrect—including true/false, matching, and fill-in-the blank. In fact, constructs in measurement theory such as reliability, validity, and the extent to which items differentiate between students who do well on a test as opposed to students who do not do well (referred to as *item discrimination*) were based initially on the assumption that items are scored as correct or incorrect (see Gulliksen, 1950; Lord & Novick, 1968; Magnusson, 1966; Nunally, 1967).

As one might expect, courses and textbooks on the topic of test construction adopted the notion of the correct/incorrect heuristic for scoring items on tests and the percentage score as the preferred summary score. From there it was a short step to assigning points to items and tasks that could not be scored correct or incorrect, such as essay items, oral presentations, and the like. Without realizing it, the world of K–12 education was soon entrenched in the point, or percentage, system.

A Conceptual Look at Assessment

The discussion thus far makes it clear that the point system as currently used in the classroom is inadequate to the task of effective formative assessment. To understand how to improve on the point system, we first must consider the basic nature of classroom assessment. It is also useful to more specifically define some terms that have been and will continue to be used throughout this book. Considering the combined works of various classroom assessment experts (McMillan, 1997; O'Connor, 1995; Stiggins, 1994, 1997; Terwilliger, 1989), the following definitions emerge:

  • *Assessment*—planned or serendipitous activities that provide information about students' understanding and skill in a specific measurement topic
  • *Test*—a type of assessment that takes place at a specific time and most commonly uses a pencil-and-paper format
  • *Evaluation*—the process of making judgments about the levels of students' understanding or skill based on an assessment
  • *Measurement*—assigning scores to an assessment based on an explicit set of rules
  • *Score*—the number or letter assigned to an assessment via the process of measurement; may be synonymous with the term *mark*

These terms provide an interesting perspective on assessment in the classroom in that they imply an integrated set of actions. An *assessment* is any planned or serendipitous activity that provides information about students' understanding and skill regarding a specific measurement topic; a *test* is one of a number of forms of assessment. Regardless of what type of assessment is used, judgments are made about each student's level of understanding and skill via the process of *evaluation*. These judgments are translated into *scores* using the process of *measurement*.

One might infer that although we typically pay attention to the final score a student receives on an assessment, we should also be cognizant of the process that was used to derive that score to ensure that it involved effective assessment, evaluation, and measurement. Underlying all of these integrated processes is the concept of *true score*.

The Concept of True Score

The concept of true score is central to virtually every aspect of measurement theory. True score is addressed more rigorously in Technical Note 3.1. Briefly, though, consider the following comments of measurement theorist David Magnusson (1966):

> The trait measured by a certain . . . test can be represented by a latent continuum, an ability scale on which every individual takes up a certain position. The position an individual takes up on the ability scale determines . . . his true score on the test, his position on the true-score scale. (p. 63)

In nontechnical terms, Magnusson's comments indicate that a student's performances on the items on a test are assumed to be *indications* only of the student's level of understanding and skill on the topic measured by the test. The student might be quite proficient in the skills and information that make up the topic being measured but miss specific items because of factors such as fatigue, misreading the items, filling in the wrong response "bubble" on an answer sheet, and so on. Conversely, the student might be quite inept at the skills and information that make up the topic being measured but provide seemingly correct answers on specific items because of factors such as guessing, cheating, luck, and so on. In short, a student's score on a particular assessment is always considered to be an estimate of the student's true score for a particular topic.

Within what is referred to as classical test theory, or CTT, the relationship between the score a student receives on a test and the student's true score on that test is represented by the following equation:

$$\text{observed score} = \text{true score} + \text{error score}$$

This equation indicates that a student's observed score on an assessment (i.e., the final score assigned by the teacher) consists of two components—the student's true score and the student's error score. The student's true score is that which represents the student's true level of understanding or skill regarding the topic being measured. The error score is the part of an observed score that is due to factors other than the student's level of understanding or skill. As we have seen in the earlier discussion, scoring assessments using points is particularly prone to error from teachers who overestimate or underestimate the points that should be assigned to items.

This inherent problem with the point system did not go unnoticed by measurement experts. Indeed, as early as 1904, renowned pioneer in educational and psychological measurement Edward Thorndike commented on the issue in the context of a spelling test. Thorndike (1904) observed:

> If one attempts to measure even so simple a thing as spelling, one is hampered by the fact that there exist no units in which to measure. One may arbitrarily make up a list of words and observe ability by the number spelled correctly. But if one examines such a list one is struck by the inequality of the units. All results based on the equality of any one word with another are necessarily inaccurate. (p. 7)

Basically, Thorndike was highlighting the fact that even with a subject area as seemingly straightforward as spelling, it is difficult, if not impossible, to assign points to individual items in a valid manner. It makes little sense to assign one point to each item because some words are harder to spell than others. However, there is also no rigorous way to assign more than one point to a single word. If spelling the word *gift* correctly is worth one point, how many points is it worth to spell the word *memento* correctly?

Item Response Theory

In spite of Thorndike's warning, the point method remained unchallenged and unchanged until about the mid-1950s, when a new theoretical basis for measurement referred to as item response theory, or IRT, was articulated. Susan Embretson and Steven Reise (2000) provide a detailed discussion of the history of IRT. Briefly, though, the initial theoretical discussion of IRT is commonly traced to the work of Allan Birnbaum (1957, 1958a, 1958b). However, the first comprehensive articulation of IRT is attributed to Frederick Lord and Melvin Novick (1968). Currently IRT is the predominant system used to design and score large-scale assessments such as tests of state standards and standardized tests.

IRT does not simply add up points to construct a score for an individual student on a given test. Rather, it uses an approach that Embretson and Reise (2000) liken to "clinical inference." They state, "In models of the clinical inference process, a potential diagnosis or inference is evaluated for plausibility. That is, given the presenting behaviors (including test behaviors), how plausible is a certain diagnosis" (p. 54). As it relates to scoring an assessment, the IRT method may be described as answering the following question: *Given this pattern of responses by the student, what is the most plausible inference as to the student's level of under-standing and skill on the trait measured by the items?* This approach is quite consis-tent with the definitions provided earlier for the terms *assessment, evaluation, measurement,* and *score.* A paper-and-pencil test is a form of assessment—a way of gathering information about students' levels of understanding and skill regard-ing a specific topic. A clinical-type inference must be made using the student's observed pattern of responses. The student's pattern of responses is what Embret-son and Reise refer to as the "presenting behavior." Evaluation is the process by which the clinical-type inference is made. Simply adding up points for correct responses and dividing by the total number of possible points is not evaluation, because no judgment is involved.

The perspective provided by IRT is a powerful one in terms of its implications for scoring classroom assessments. First, it adds credibility to the assertion that it is impossible (for all practical purposes) to devise a valid scheme that classroom teachers could use to assign points to items. Second, it implies a basic strategy that classroom teachers can use to design and score classroom assessments as reli-ably as possible with the caveat that there is no perfectly reliable way to score an assessment, whether it be constructed by a teacher, a district, a state, or a testing company.

Understanding the Logic of IRT

If IRT models don't add up points to compute a student's score on a test, what process do they use, and how does it apply to a teacher scoring a classroom assess-ment? We begin with the process used by IRT models.

IRT models operate from some basic assumptions (see Technical Note 3.2). First, they assume that the topic measured by a given test is not observable directly. IRT theorists typically talk about "latent" traits. Next, they assume that the latent trait being measured follows a normal distribution like that depicted in Figure 3.4, which is familiar to many educators as well as the general public (see Technical Note 3.3 for a discussion of the normal distribution). Note that in this depiction, the average score is 0 and the range of scores goes from −3 to +3. Thus, the score one receives on a test based on IRT is +3, +2, +1, 0, and so on, referred to as "trait scores." These trait scores are then translated to some other metric. For example, the metric might be 1,000 points. Thus, a score of +3 might translate to a score of 1,000, a score of 2 might translate to 750, a score of 0 might translate to 500, and so on.

To determine a person's trait score, IRT models use sophisticated mathemat-ics to analyze patterns of item responses (for a discussion, see Embretson & Reise,

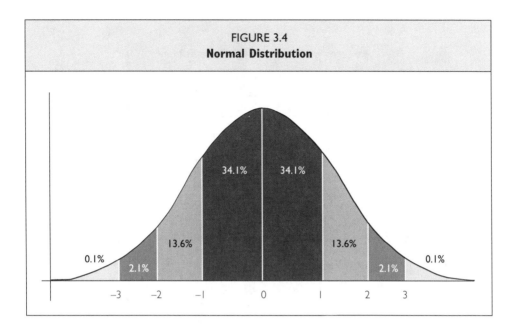

FIGURE 3.4
Normal Distribution

2000). For example, assume that a nine-item test has been designed using IRT theory. (In practice, many more items are used in IRT test development.) Also assume that when the test was being developed, it was determined mathematically that items 1, 2, and 3 represented very easy information about the trait being measured; items 4, 5, and 6 represented information of moderate difficulty; and items 7, 8, and 9 represented relatively difficult information.

With this information as a backdrop, various patterns of responses on the nine test items can be assigned trait scores. For example, consider Figure 3.5, which depicts the pattern of responses for three students across the nine test items. In the figure, a *1* indicates that the student answered the item correctly, whereas a *0* indicates that the student did not answer the item correctly. Notice that all three students answered six items correctly. However, using the information about difficulty level of each item, an IRT model will compute the probability of each pattern as it relates to each possible trait score depicted in Figure 3.5. It will then assign the trait score that is most probable, given the observed pattern. For Student A, the IRT model has computed the probability of this pattern of responses for a trait score of –3.0, –2.5, –2.0, –1.5, and so on. The mathematics of the IRT model determined that the trait score of +0.5 has the highest probability, given the pattern of responses. The same analytic logic and mathematics assigned trait scores of +1.0 and +1.5 to Students B and C, respectively.

FIGURE 3.5
Patterns of Responses for Three Students

Item	Student		
	A	B	C
1	1	1	1
2	1	1	0
3	1	0	1
4	1	0	0
5	1	1	1
6	0	1	0
7	1	1	1
8	0	0	1
9	0	1	1
Total Score	6	6	6
Hypothetical IRT Trait Score	+0.5	+1.0	+1.5

Although this example is contrived and a gross oversimplification of the IRT process, it illustrates the underlying logic of IRT test development—that of assigning a trait score that has the highest probability or is the most reasonable, given what is known about the difficulty of each item and a student's pattern of responses on those items. To use the logic of IRT to score classroom assessments, two elements must be in place:

• A scale that represents performance along a continuum for a given trait
• A process to translate patterns of responses on assessments into scores on the scale

We begin with the scale.

A Scale That Represents Performance Along a Continuum

IRT models assume that performance on a given latent trait follows a normal distribution like that shown in Figure 3.4, and the models use complex mathematics to translate a student's pattern of responses to a trait score on that distribution. Obviously classroom teachers don't have the luxury of complex mathematical calculations when scoring an assessment. Consequently, they need a scale that is

---

FIGURE 3.6
Scoring Scale Representing Progress on a Measurement Topic

Topic Score on Scale	Description of Place on Scale
4.0	In addition to Score 3.0 performance, in-depth inferences and applications that go beyond what was taught
3.5	In addition to Score 3.0 performance, partial success at inferences and applications that go beyond what was taught
3.0	No major errors or omissions regarding any of the information and/or processes (simple or complex) that were explicitly taught
2.5	No major errors or omissions regarding the simpler details and processes and partial knowledge of the more complex ideas and processes
2.0	No major errors or omissions regarding the simpler details and processes but major errors or omissions regarding the more complex ideas and processes
1.5	Partial knowledge of the simpler details and processes but major errors or omissions regarding the more complex ideas and processes
1.0	With help, a partial understanding of some of the simpler details and processes and some of the more complex ideas and processes
0.5	With help, a partial understanding of some of the simpler details and processes but not the more complex ideas and processes
0.0	Even with help, no understanding or skill demonstrated

based not on the normal distribution but on a logical progression of understanding and skill for a specific measurement topic. Figure 3.6 represents one such scale.

To illustrate the scale shown in Figure 3.6, consider the science measurement topic of heredity. The lowest score value on the scale is a 0.0, representing no knowledge of the topic; even with help the student demonstrates no understanding or skill relative to the topic of heredity. A score of 1.0 indicates that *with help* the student shows partial knowledge of the simpler details and processes as well as the more complex ideas and processes. The notion of providing help to students on an assessment is an important feature of the scale that is addressed in depth later in this chapter. To be assigned a score of 2.0, the student *independently* demonstrates understanding of and skill at the simpler details and processes but not the more complex ideas and processes. A score of 3.0 indicates that the student demonstrates understanding of and skill at all the content—simple and complex—*that was taught in class.* However, a score of 4.0 indicates that the student

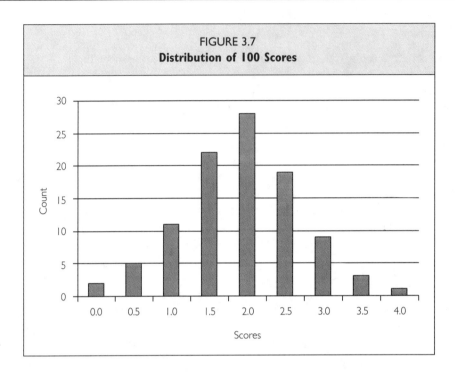

FIGURE 3.7
Distribution of 100 Scores

demonstrates inferences and applications that *go beyond what was taught in class*. This, too, is an important feature of the scale that is addressed in depth in Chapter 4. Here the scale is introduced as a logical alternative to an IRT continuum based on the normal distribution shown in Figure 3.4.

Interestingly, when the scale in Figure 3.6 is used to score students' assessments, the distribution of scores strongly resembles a normal distribution. To illustrate, consider Figure 3.7, which shows the distribution of 100 student assessments scored using the scale in Figure 3.6. The similarity to a normal distribution is a partial indication that the scale is sensitive to the true variation in students' scores for a given topic. That is, if the true scores for a group of students are distributed normally, a scale that results in a distribution that resembles the normal distribution is probably sensitive to the students' true scores (see Technical Note 3.3 for a discussion).

Translating Patterns of Responses on Assessments into Scores on the Scale

The second item necessary to use the logic of IRT to score classroom assessments is a process for translating patterns of responses on an assessment into scores on the scale. Perhaps the best way to understand the process is to introduce it in the context of a typical classroom assessment, such as the one shown here.

....

You are thinking of renting a car and have looked at the rates for four companies. Each company has a set daily rate and a certain amount of free mileage. However, once you've used up your free miles with each company, they charge per mile in addition to the daily rate.

	Red-Bird Rental	Easy Rental	Reliable Rental	M&A Rental
Daily Rate	$43.00	$27.50	$40.00	$35.25
Free Mileage	1,200	500	900	800
Cost per Mile	$0.22/mile	$0.32/mile	$0.25/mile	$0.20/mile

Section I:
  1. Which company has the highest daily rate?
       Answer _____

  2. Which company has the most free mileage?
       Answer _____

  3. If each company had the same daily rate and the same amount of free mileage, which would be the cheapest?
       Answer _____

  4. If each company had the same amount of free mileage and the same cost per mile, which company would be the most expensive?
       Answer _____

  5. Once you've used up your free mileage, which company would cost the least amount of money to travel 100 miles in a single day?
       Answer _____

Section II:
  6. If you travel 100 miles per day, which company is the least expensive for

          5 days: Answer _____
         10 days: Answer _____

15 days: Answer _____
20 days: Answer _____

Create a table or a graph that shows how expensive each company is for each of the four options above (5 days, 10 days, 15 days, 20 days), and explain how you calculated your answers.

Section III:

7. Each of the four companies could be considered the "best deal" under certain conditions. For each company, describe the situation under which it would be the best selection. In your answer and explanation, use the daily rate, free mileage, and the rate per mile after free mileage.

....

The first thing to notice about the test is that it involves different types of items. Items 1 through 5 are fairly simple; they require students to read the table and make a few simple calculations. I refer to such items as Type I items—those that deal with basic details and processes that are relatively easy for students. Item 6 is much more complex than items 1 through 5; students must make multiple calculations and compare the results of those calculations. I refer to items like this as Type II items—those that address complex ideas and processes that are more difficult for students. Typically these items require students to generate something that is not obvious. In this case, students must compute the total cost for each company for differing amounts of rental time and then compare total costs for each company. Finally, item 7 asks students to make unique inferences or applications of content typically not addressed in class. I refer to items like this as Type III items.

The inclusion of Type I, II, and III items on this assessment is not coincidental. An examination of the scale in Figure 3.6 demonstrates that Type I items are required to determine if students have attained a score of 2.0, indicating that they are competent on the simpler details and processes. Type II items are required to determine if students have attained a score of 3.0, indicating that they are competent on the more complex ideas and processes. Type III items are necessary to determine if students have attained a score of 4.0, indicating that they can go beyond what was presented in class.

In summary, to design a classroom assessment that can be scored using the scale in Figure 3.6, three types of items must be included:

• **Type I items** that address basic details and processes that are relatively easy for students

- **Type II items** that address more complex ideas and processes and are more difficult for students
- **Type III items** that go beyond what was taught in class

In Chapter 4 we will consider in depth how to design these three types of items. However, I have found that teachers understand the three item types intuitively and are quite adept at constructing them even without a great deal of training regarding their characteristics.

Using the Simplified Scale

Given that an assessment contains the three types of items just discussed, it is relatively easy for a teacher to translate patterns of responses into scale scores for a measurement topic. When teachers are using this system for the first time, I commonly recommend they start with a simplified version of the scale, as shown in Figure 3.8. Figure 3.8 is referred to as the "simplified scale" because it contains five whole-point values only—4.0, 3.0, 2.0, 1.0, and 0.0. Although this scale is less precise than the scale with half-point scores (3.5, 2.5, 1.5, and 0.5), it serves as a good introduction to the process of translating item response patterns into scale scores. Additionally, in some situations half-point scores are difficult to discern or simply don't make much sense.

FIGURE 3.8	
Simplified Scoring Scale	
Topic Score on Scale	**Description of Place on Scale**
4.0	In addition to Score 3.0 performance, in-depth inferences and applications that go beyond what was taught
3.0	No major errors or omissions regarding any of the information and/or processes (simple or complex) that were explicitly taught
2.0	No major errors or omissions regarding the simpler details and processes but major errors or omissions regarding the more complex ideas and processes
1.0	With help, a partial understanding of some of the simpler details and processes and some of the more complex ideas and processes
0.0	Even with help, no understanding or skill demonstrated

Source: From Marzano (2004c). Copyright © 2004 by Marzano & Associates. Reprinted with permission. All rights reserved.

FIGURE 3.9 Quick Reference Guide for the Simplified Scoring Scale					
Student Pattern of Responses					
Type I Items	+	+	+	some understanding with help	0 with help
Type II Items	+	+	0	some understanding with help	0 with help
Type III Items	+	0	0	0 with help	0 with help
Score on Simplified (5-point) Scale	4.0	3.0	2.0	1.0	0.0

Note: + indicates a correct response. 0 indicates incorrect or no response.
Source: From Marzano (2004c). Copyright © 2004 by Marzano & Associates. All rights reserved. Adapted with permission.

To illustrate how to use the simplified scale, assume a student answered all the Type I items correctly (items 1 through 5), as well as the Type II item (item 6), but she missed the Type III item (item 7). The student would be assigned a score of 3.0 because her pattern of responses on the items indicates that she understands the simpler details as well as the more complex ideas but does not make inferences and applications beyond what was taught.

Figure 3.9 provides teachers with a quick reference to scoring assessments using the simplified scale. In the figure, the symbol + indicates that the student responded correctly to a particular item type (Type I, II, III); the symbol 0 indicates that the student responded incorrectly or provided no response; and the words *some understanding with help* indicate that the teacher provided the student with guidance and clues and the student exhibited some knowledge of the content addressed in the items. Thus, Figure 3.9 indicates that students who answer all items correctly receive a score of 4.0 on the assessment. Students who answer all Type I and Type II items correctly but do not answer Type III items correctly receive a score of 3.0. Students who answer Type I items correctly but do not answer Type II and Type III items correctly receive a score of 2.0. If students answer no items correctly while working independently, but with help receive partial credit on Type I and Type II items, then they receive a score of 1.0. Finally, students who answer no items correctly while working independently and still cannot do so with help receive a score of 0.0.

The representation in Figure 3.9 highlights again the important distinction between a score of 0.0 and 1.0. To discern whether a student should receive a score of 1.0 or 0.0, a teacher must interact with the student, because for both score values the student provides no correct responses to any of the items on the assessment. At first glance the assessments for the student who deserves a 1.0 and the student who deserves a 0.0 look the same. Nothing appears correct. However, if a student can answer some items correctly when provided with help or guidance by the teacher, the student receives a score of 1.0. If the student cannot answer any items correctly even with help, the student receives a score of 0.0.

At times when I have presented the idea of meeting with individual students regarding their responses on a test, some teachers have rightfully questioned how they can be expected to do so when they have 150 students or more. The simple answer is that they must interact only with those students who answer no items correctly or those who do not even attempt to answer any items. As shown in Figure 3.7 (the distribution representing the scores of 100 students on a test), few students typically receive scores of 0.0 and 1.0. In general, then, a teacher must meet with a small group of students—only those who provide no response or answer all items incorrectly.

As mentioned previously, I have found that once teachers become familiar with the simplified scale depicted in Figure 3.8, they can score classroom assessments quickly and accurately. To do so, a teacher reads each student's responses to each item, marking the responses as correct or incorrect using a simple system like a plus sign (+) for correctly answered items and a zero (0) for incorrectly answered items and items for which a student has provided no response. Going back to our sample test, the teacher marks each item with a + or a 0. Assume that a student has a + for items 1 through 5 and a 0 for items 6 and 7. Keeping in mind that items 1 through 5 are Type I, item 6 is Type II, and item 7 is Type III, the teacher then interprets the pattern of responses using the quick reference guide shown in Figure 3.9.

Additionally, some teachers have found the flowchart shown in Figure 3.10 to be quite helpful. It shows the decisions a teacher might make when scoring an assessment. After coding the items on a test as correct or incorrect, the teacher begins by (metaphorically) asking if there are any major errors or omissions in the Type II items. If the answer is yes, the teacher asks if there are any major errors or omissions in the Type I items. If the answer is no, then the student's score is at least a 2.0, and so on. Although the scheme is implied in the scale

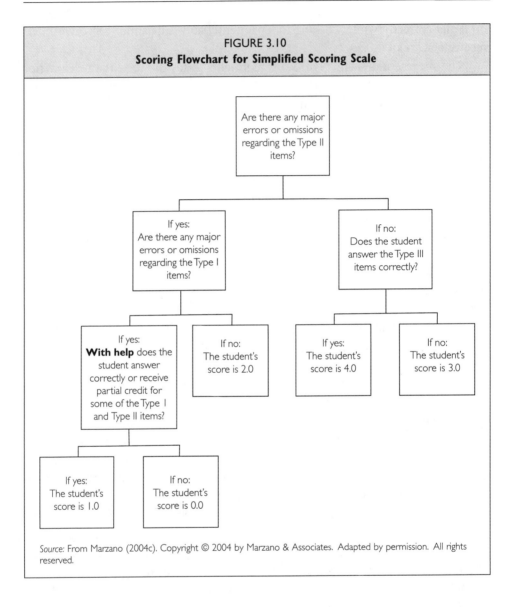

FIGURE 3.10
Scoring Flowchart for Simplified Scoring Scale

itself, I have found that the flowchart demonstrates the underlying "logic" of this scoring system. Recall from Figure 1.2 in Chapter 1 that scoring classroom assessments using a set of rules is associated with a 32-percentile-point gain in student achievement (Fuchs & Fuchs, 1986). The flowchart in Figure 3.10 depicts a rather tight system of rules.

Using the Complete Scale

The simplified scale is a good place to start when first trying the system described in this chapter. However, measurement theory tells us that the more values a scale has, the more precise the measurement. Relative to IRT models, Embretson and Reise (2000) explain: "Decreasing interval size increases precision in estimating level" (p. 56). To illustrate, assume that a teacher used a scale with only two values—pass/fail—to score a test. Also assume that to pass the test a student had to answer 60 percent of the items correctly. In this scenario the student who answered all items correctly would receive the same score (pass) as the student who answered 60 percent of the items correctly. Similarly, the student who answered no items correctly would receive the same score (fail) as the student who answered 59 percent of the items correctly. The pass/fail scores on this test would not provide the teacher or the students with a great deal of information about student performance. By inference, then, we can conclude that the complete scale with half-point scores will provide more precise measurement than the simplified version with whole-point values only.

Figure 3.11 shows the complete scale again, this time in a format more useful for scoring assessments. The half-point scores are set off to the right to signify that they describe response patterns between the whole-point scores and, therefore, allow for more precision when scoring an assessment. Specifically, the half-point scores allow for partial credit to be assigned to items. To illustrate, consider the scores of 3.0, 2.5, and 2.0. A score of 3.0 indicates that the student has answered all Type I items correctly (those involving simpler details and processes), as well as all Type II items (those involving more complex ideas and processes). A score of 2.0 indicates that the student has answered all Type I items correctly but has missed all Type II items. However, what score should be assigned if a student has answered all Type I items correctly and some Type II items correctly or has received partial credit on the Type II items? Using the simplified scale, we would have to assign a score of 2.0. Using the complete scale, a score value of 2.5 would be assigned. This allows for much more precise measurement.

As mentioned previously, sometimes it is difficult to assign half-point scores. For example, when scoring a student's ability to carry out a specific technique in a dance class, it might be difficult to think in terms of half-point scores. If the student can perform the basic steps in the technique but has trouble with the more complex steps, it might be hard to think in terms of "partial credit" for the more complex steps—either she can do them or she can't. The same restriction might

---

FIGURE 3.11
Complete Scoring Scale

Topic Score on Scale	Description of Place on Scale
4.0	**In addition to Score 3.0 performance, in-depth inferences and applications that go beyond what was taught**
3.5	In addition to Score 3.0 performance, partial success at inferences and applications that go beyond what was taught
3.0	**No major errors or omissions regarding any of the information and/or processes (simple or complex) that were explicitly taught**
2.5	No major errors or omissions regarding the simpler details and process and partial knowledge of the more complex ideas and processes
2.0	**No major errors or omissions regarding the simpler details and processes but major errors or omissions regarding the more complex ideas and processes**
1.5	Partial knowledge of the simpler details and processes but major errors or omissions regarding the more complex ideas and procedures
1.0	**With help, a partial understanding of some of the simpler details and processes and some of the more complex ideas and processes**
0.5	With help, a partial understanding of some of the simpler details and processes but not the more complex ideas and processes
0.0	**Even with help, no understanding or skill demonstrated**

Source: From Marzano (2004c). Copyright © 2004 by Marzano & Associates. All rights reserved. Adapted by permission.

---

apply to scoring a student's ability to use a specific type of tool in a mechanics class or to perform a specific skill in a physical education class.

The complete scale, then, is a logical extension of the simplified scale. Teachers can use the two scales interchangeably. When the type of assessment allows for determining partial credit, the complete scale is preferable. When the type of assessment does not allow for determining partial credit, the simplified scale is used.

Figure 3.12 depicts the relationship between the two scales in terms of scoring. As before, the symbol + indicates that the student responded correctly to a particular item type (I, II, III); the symbol 0 indicates that the student responded incorrectly or provided no response; the term *part* indicates that the student responded correctly to some of the items or answered some parts of the items correctly. (Appendix A contains another comparison of the complete scale and the simplified scale, although that in Figure 3.12 suffices for most people.)

FIGURE 3.12
Relationship Between Simplified and Complete Scoring Scales

	Student Pattern of Responses								
Type I Items	+	+	+	+	+	part	part with help	part with help	0 with help
Type II Items	+	+	+	part	0	0	part with help	0 with help	0 with help
Type III Items	+	part	0	0	0	0	0 with help	0 with help	0 with help
Score on Complete (9-Point) Scale	4.0	3.5	3.0	2.5	2.0	1.5	1.0	0.5	0.0
Score on Simplified (5-Point) Scale	4.0	3.0			2.0		1.0		0.0

Note: + indicates a correct response. 0 indicates incorrect or no response.
Source: From Marzano (2004c). Copyright © 2004 by Marzano & Associates. All rights reserved. Adapted by permission.

As before, to score a classroom assessment using the complete scale, a teacher examines a student's responses and marks them as correct (+), incorrect/ no response (0), or partially correct (*part*). Going back to the sample test, the teacher would mark each item using the symbols +, *0*, or *part*. Assume that a student has + for all Type I items and a combination of +, 0, and *part* for the Type II items. The student would receive a score of 2.5. As another example, assume that a student answers no items correctly. However, when the teacher provides the student with some clues, the student demonstrates partial credit for the Type I items but not the Type II items. She receives a score of 0.5. As before, some teachers have found the flowchart in Figure 3.13 to be helpful in demonstrating the logic of scoring assessments using the complete scale. To use the flowchart, the teacher again begins by asking the question, are there any major errors or omissions on the Type II items? If the answer is yes, the teacher asks the question, are there any major errors or omissions regarding the Type I items? If the answer is no, the teacher asks the question, does the student have partial credit

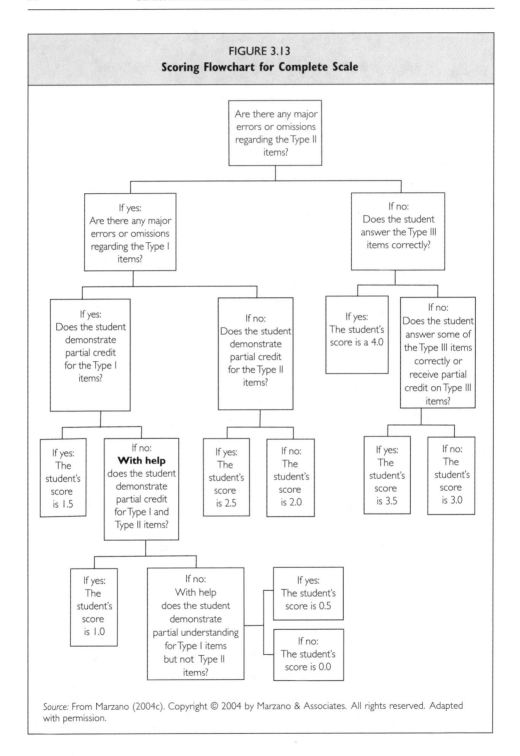

FIGURE 3.13
Scoring Flowchart for Complete Scale

on the Type II items? If the answer is yes, the student's score is 2.5. If the answer is no, the student's score is 2.0, and so on.

What to Do If Student Responses Don't Follow a Logical Pattern

One issue that might occasionally arise is that a student's response patterns don't follow the expected patterns for the simplified scale or the complete scale. That is, a student exhibits an illogical response pattern, such as answering all Type II items correctly but missing some of the Type I items; or answering the Type III items correctly but missing some of the Type II items, and so on. The first thing to note is that this phenomenon occurs even with standardized tests that have been designed rigorously using IRT models (see Embretson & Reise, 2000). Within IRT parlance, illogical response patterns are referred to as "aberrant patterns." The second thing to note is that an illogical response pattern might occur for a number of reasons, including the following:

- The items in the test were flawed in some way.
- Students put effort into answering some items but not others.
- The teacher's evaluations of the student's responses are inaccurate.

A teacher can do a number of things in such situations, including dropping some items because they are deemed to be invalid, rethinking the classification of specific items, and meeting individually with students who demonstrate illogical response patterns. This issue is covered in more depth in Chapter 4. However, here I simply note that the ultimate goal when scoring any assessment is to estimate each student's true score on the topic being assessed as accurately as possible using the complete scale or the simplified scale. Realizing that no assessment can ever provide perfectly accurate data about a student, it behooves the teacher to go beyond the observed response patterns by collecting more information.

This notion that one must go beyond a simple tallying of correct and incorrect answers to interpret a test score is the subject of much discussion among measurement experts. In fact, in his 2005 presidential address to the National Council on Measurement in Education, David Frisbie (2005) explained that for decades educators have mistakenly thought of reliability as being a characteristic of a specific test. He explained that reliability is more properly thought of as the manner in which scores are interpreted. (See Technical Note 3.4 for a more detailed discussion of Frisbie's comments.) At face value an implication of Frisbie's comments is that numerical scores on tests are never reliable in themselves. When the scores don't make sense, educators must look beyond them to obtain the most accurate estimate of students' true scores.

The Accuracy of This Method of Scoring Classroom Assessment

A logical and important question regarding the method of scoring assessments described in this chapter is, how accurate is it? As mentioned in the previous section, Technical Note 3.4 addresses the concept of *reliability* in more depth. Briefly, though, reliability can be thought of as how precisely students' scores on assessments estimate their true scores. Typically, some type of reliability coefficient is computed for a test; these reliability coefficients range from 0 to 1.0, with 1.0 indicating a perfect reliability.

To examine the reliability of the system described in this chapter, five teachers scored the same 10 students' science tests discussed at the beginning of this chapter. These five teachers were as familiar with the test content as were those teachers who scored the test using the point system. However, this second set of five teachers used an early version of the simplified scale shown in Figure 3.8. In effect, then, five teachers scored the test by assigning points, and five teachers scored the test using the simplified scale. (See Marzano, 2002a, for details.) A reliability coefficient (technically referred to as a *generalizability coefficient*) was computed for the point system and the system using the simplified scale. The reliability coefficient using the point system was .294, whereas the reliability coefficient using the simplified scale was .719. Additionally, it was found that if two teachers independently scored a student's test using the simplified scale, the combined score for those two independent ratings had an estimated reliability (generalizability) of .822. If four teachers independently scored a student's assessment, the combined score for those four independent ratings had a reliability of .901. Similar findings have been reported by Michael Flicek (2005a, 2005b).

These findings are quite promising because they indicate that under the right conditions, teacher-made assessments can have reliabilities that are in line with those reported for standardized tests. To illustrate, Jason Osborne (2003) found that the average reliability reported in psychology journals is .83. Lou and colleagues (1996) reported a typical reliability on standardized achievement tests of .85 and a reliability of .75 for unstandardized tests of academic achievement.

Since the initial studies conducted using the simplified scale, other studies have demonstrated that the complete scale produces even better results (Marzano, 2006). Additionally, these studies indicate that the complete scale is most useful and accurate when it is rewritten to identify the specific aspects of measurement topics that signify scores of 2.0, 3.0, and 4.0. To illustrate, consider Figure 3.14. The scale in the figure is for the measurement topic of *reading for*

FIGURE 3.14
Scoring Scale Written for a Specific Measurement Topic

Subject Area: Language Arts	
Measurement Topic: Reading for Main Idea	
Grade 5	
Score 4.0	In addition to Score 3.0 performance, the student goes beyond what was taught by • Explaining which parts of a pattern are explicit and which parts must be inferred. • Explaining and defending inferences regarding patterns.
	Score 3.5 In addition to Score 3.0 performance, partial success at inferences and applications that go beyond what was taught.
Score 3.0	While reading grade-appropriate material, the student identifies the main pattern of ideas, such as • Complex causal relationships that are explicit and implied. • Complex chronologies that are explicit and implied. • Problems with basic solutions that are explicit and implied. • Plots with single story lines that are explicit and implied. The student exhibits no major errors or omissions.
	Score 2.5 No major errors or omissions regarding the simpler details and processes, and partial knowledge of the more complex ideas and processes.
Score 2.0	The student makes no major errors or omissions regarding the simpler details, such as identifying • Complex causal relationships that are explicit. • Complex chronologies that are explicit. • Problems with basic solutions that are explicit. • Plots with single story lines that are explicit. However, the student exhibits major errors or omissions on the more complex ideas and processes.
	Score 1.5 Partial knowledge of the simpler details and processes but major errors or omissions regarding the more complex ideas and procedures.
Score 1.0	With help, the student demonstrates a partial understanding of some of the simpler details and processes and some of the more complex ideas and processes.
	Score 0.5 With help, a partial understanding of some of the simpler details and processes but not the more complex ideas and processes.
Score 0.0	Even with help, the student demonstrates no understanding or skill.

main idea at the 5th grade level. Note that specific elements have been provided for the score values 4.0, 3.0, and 2.0. It is important to note that the example in Figure 3.14 is just that—an example. Many schemes might be used to define and articulate the specific elements of score values 4.0, 3.0, and 2.0 (for a discussion, see Marzano & Haystead, in press). In this example, a score of 3.0 indicates that a student can identify specific types of organizational patterns whether they are explicitly stated in the text or implied. The score value of 2.0 indicates that the student can identify the same type of patterns if they are explicitly stated in the text but makes major errors or omissions when those patterns are implied. A score value of 4.0 indicates that in addition to identifying explicit and implied patterns the student can explain and defend inferences about those patterns.

I believe that the format shown in Figure 3.14 is the optimal way to construct measurement topics. To this end, Appendix B presents the language arts measurement topic shown in the figure for various grade levels as a general example for districts and schools to follow. For a complete listing of measurement topics for language arts, mathematics, science, and social studies, see *Making Standards Useful to Classroom Teachers* (Marzano & Haystead, in press). I believe that one of the most powerful actions a district or school can take is to articulate each measurement topic at each grade level in the format shown in Figure 3.14. Such action not only requires the district or school to rigorously define expected levels of performance for each measurement topic, but it also provides teachers with explicit guidance for scoring assessments.

The Issue of Performance Standards

To be used effectively to track students' progress on measurement topics, the scale presented in this chapter must conform to current conventions of standards-based reporting. One of those conventions is to identify performance standards for student achievement. Unfortunately, the concept of a performance standard is frequently misunderstood. The term was popularized in the 1993 report to the National Education Goals Panel (1993) by the Goal 3 and 4 Standards Review Planning Group. Commonly referred to as the Malcom Report in deference to Shirley M. Malcom, chair of the planning group, the report defined *performance standards* as "how good is good enough" (pp. ii–iii). Since the publication of that report, a convention that has caught on across the United States is to define student performance in terms of four categories: *advanced, proficient, basic,* and *below basic.* This scheme has it roots in the work of the National Assessment of Educational Progress. As James Popham (2003) notes:

> Increasingly, U.S. educators are building performance standards along the lines of the descriptive categories used in the National Assessment of Educational Progress (NAEP), a test administered periodically under the auspices of the federal government. NAEP results permit students' performances in participating states to be compared . . . [S]ince 1990, NAEP results have been described in four performance categories: *advanced, proficient, basic,* and *below basic.* Most of the 50 states now use those four categories or labels quite similar to them. For example, if students were taking a statewide examination consisting of 65 multiple-choice items, the performance standards for the test could be set by deciding how many of the 65 items must be answered correctly for a student to be classified as *advanced,* how many items for *proficient* and so on. (p. 39)

The complete scale presented in this chapter can easily be adapted to conform to this convention. To illustrate, consider Figure 3.15. The logic of the categorization scheme used in the figure is straightforward. *Advanced* performance means that a student can go beyond what was presented in class, indicated by the score values of 4.0 and 3.5. *Proficient* performance means that a student exhibits no errors relative to the simple and complex ideas and processes, or the student exhibits no errors regarding the simpler details and processes and partial knowledge of more complex ideas and processes, indicated by the score values of 3.0 and 2.5, and so on.

Although the logic of Figure 3.15 is straightforward, it is useful to keep in mind that the "cut point" for each performance level is quite arbitrary. Again, Popham (2003) notes:

> My point is that performance standards are malleable, and you never know what something like "basic" means until you read the fine-print description of that level of performance. For example, the No Child Left Behind Act calls for states to establish at least three levels of academic achievement standards (*advanced, proficient,* and *basic*) and to demonstrate, over time, state-decreed increases in the proportion of students deemed "proficient" or above. . . . However, each state is allowed to define "proficient" in its own way. And because there are significant negative sanctions for schools that fail to get enough students to score at the proficient levels on NCLB tests, in some states there have been *remarkably* lenient levels of "proficiency" established. (p. 40)

One useful interpretation of Popham's message is that districts and schools should set performance standards that reflect expectations about students that the district or school deem reasonable and valuable. For example, a district or a school might decide that the *below basic* category should end at the score value of 1.5 as opposed to the value of 1.0, or that it should end at 0.5 instead of 1.0.

FIGURE 3.15		
Complete Scoring Scale Adapted to NAEP Performance Levels		
Advanced	**Score 4.0:**	**In addition to Score 3.0 performance, in-depth inferences and applications that go beyond what was taught**
	Score 3.5:	In addition to Score 3.0 performance, partial success at inferences and applications that go beyond what was taught
Proficient	**Score 3.0:**	**No major errors or omissions regarding any of the information and/or processes (simple or complex) that were explicitly taught**
	Score 2.5:	No major errors or omissions regarding the simpler details and processes and partial knowledge of the more complex ideas and processes
Basic	**Score 2.0:**	**No major errors or omissions regarding the simpler details and processes, but major errors or omissions regarding the more complex ideas and processes**
	Score 1.5:	Partial knowledge of the simpler details and processes, but major errors or omissions regarding the more complex ideas and processes
Below Basic	**Score 1.0:**	**With help, a partial understanding of some of the simpler details and processes and some of the more complex ideas and processes**
	Score 0.5:	With help, a partial understanding of some of the simpler details and processes but not the more complex ideas and processes
	Score 0.0:	**Even with help, no understanding or skill demonstrated**

Source: From Marzano (2004c). Copyright © 2004 by Marzano & Associates. All rights reserved. Adapted by permission.

Summary and Conclusions

An argument can be made against using the point method for scoring assessments. An alternative approach is grounded in the logic of item response theory. Using this approach, teachers translate student response patterns into scores on a scale that represents progression of understanding and skill for a given measurement topic. A simplified version of the scale uses whole-point scores only. A complete version of the scale allows for half-point scores and consequently more precise measurement.

Designing
Classroom Assessments

Chapter 3 presented a process for scoring assessments that is very different from the traditional point system. Within that new system, response patterns for students are used to determine each student's score on a scale that represents expected growth milestones for a measurement topic. This chapter describes how to design assessments that fit this new approach. This chapter also addresses how a teacher should plan for the formative assessments that will be used throughout a grading period. In terms of the research-based generalizations discussed in Chapter 1, this chapter helps put into operation the third and fourth generalizations—that classroom assessment should be formative and frequent. We begin with the issue of planning assessments for a grading period.

Designing a Formative Assessment System

The first questions a teacher should answer are, how many measurement topics will be addressed during a grading period and how many assessments will be administered for each measurement topic? For example, during the first quarter of the school year, a 7th grade science teacher might wish to keep track of student progress on the following six topics:

1. Matter and Energy
2. Force and Motion
3. Reproduction and Heredity
4. Scientific Investigations and Communications
5. The Earth and the Processes That Shape It
6. Adaptation and Interdependence of Life

Presumably the district or school has determined that these measurement topics will be the focus of instruction for the first nine weeks of 7th grade. Most probably the teacher would also wish to or be required to keep track of some life skill topics such as class participation, work completion, working in groups, and behavior. We consider these topics later in the chapter.

It would be fairly inefficient to use independent assessments for each science topic. Using independent assessments for each topic would also probably not fit well with the teacher's instructional practices. That is, during the first few weeks of the quarter, the teacher might want to address the topics of (1) matter and energy and (2) force and motion. It would make better sense to design assessments that addressed both of these topics than individual assessments for each. Each assessment would receive two scores, one for each topic.

Planning an assessment system, then, for a grading period involves identifying which topics will be assessed, when they will be assessed, and whether a specific assessment will address more than one topic. Although a teacher does not have to identify every assessment that will be used for each measurement topic for a grading period, it is useful to "rough out" a general plan. For example, Figure 4.1 depicts a general plan for assessing the six science topics over a nine-week period. As shown in the figure, the teacher has planned to focus on topics 1, 2, and 3 in the first three weeks. During this time she will assess each topic twice. During the

Week	Topic					
	1	2	3	4	5	6
1	X	X				
2		X	X			
3	X		X			
4				X		X
5					X	
6				X	X	X
7	X	X	X			
8				X	X	X
9	X	X	X	X	X	X

FIGURE 4.1
General Plan for Assessing Six Measurement Topics over Nine Weeks

first week she will assess topics 1 and 2, perhaps with a single assessment that includes items for both topics. In the second week she will assess topics 2 and 3, perhaps with a single test or separate tests for each topic. In the third week she will assess topics 1 and 3. In the next three weeks she will address measurement topics 4, 5, and 6. Again, she assesses each topic twice. Note that in the final week she will assess all six topics, perhaps with a comprehensive final examination.

Although Figure 4.1 presents an assessment scheme for nine weeks, it is not uncommon for teachers to organize topics into "units" of instruction that do not extend over the entire grading period. Benjamin Bloom (1976) may have been the first person to describe this behavior in teachers when he noted that during a year of school, students encounter about 150 separate "learning units," each representing about seven hours of direct schoolwork. Assuming that the school day is divided into five academic courses, students may encounter about 30 units within a year-long course (or about 15 learning units within a semester-long course). The unit approach is quite amenable to planning in the manner shown in Figure 4.1 in that some topics might naturally cluster together to form instructional units. For example, the first three topics might cluster together to form a four-and-a-half-week unit, and the last three topics might cluster together to form a similar unit.

A movement that is gaining popularity across the United States is for a school or district to design assessments for specific measurement topics that all teachers must use. Larry Ainsworth and Donald Viegut (2006) chronicle the design and use of such assessments. Sometimes referred to as "common assessments" or "benchmark assessments," they are typically administered at the end of a grading period (e.g., at the end of nine weeks or at the end of each semester). To illustrate, assume that a school-level committee of science teachers has designed assessments for each of the six science topics identified earlier, to be administered at the end of a grading period. The teacher who designed the scheme in Figure 4.1 could then use those assessments as her final examination during week 9 instead of designing her own final examination.

This approach has a number of advantages. First, every science teacher who teaches these topics would use the same final examination, thus ensuring that all teachers use the same scoring protocols. Second, as explained in Chapter 3, when two teachers score an assessment using the system presented in this book, the reliability of the combined score from the two teachers has been found to be as high as .82 (see Marzano, 2002a). Thus, if two science teachers independently scored each final examination and each student's score on the examination was computed by averaging the two independent scores, the reliability of those jointly scored assessments might rival the reliabilities of some state-level tests—not to mention the fact that joint scoring of student assessments is one of the most powerful forms of professional development available to teachers (see Ainsworth & Viegut, 2006). In short, common assessments for measurement topics can be a powerful addition to the system of formative assessments presented in this book.

Teacher-Designed Assessments

Once teachers have articulated an assessment scheme, they must construct the assessments (except, of course, for the common, school- or district-designed assessments they will use). Construction of the assessments does not have to be accomplished before the beginning of the unit or grading period. Over the years I have observed that teachers typically construct their assessments a week (or less) ahead of time.

As discussed in Chapter 3, the ideal assessment involves three types of items or tasks:

   • **Type I items or tasks**, which address basic details and processes that are relatively easy for students

   • **Type II items or tasks**, which address more complex ideas and processes

   • **Type III items or tasks**, which require students to make inferences or applications that go beyond what was taught in class

Note that the descriptions of these three types use the terms *items* and *tasks*. I use these terms somewhat interchangeably throughout the remainder of the text. In general, though, an *item* refers to the traditional multiple-choice, fill-in-the-blank, true/false, and short-answer formats that are common in assessments. The term *task* refers to more robust ways of gathering information from students regarding their status on a given topic, such as a performance task, demonstrations, and even questions asked by the teacher in informal settings.

I have found that teachers can construct items and tasks for each of the three types quite intuitively. To illustrate, assume that a 6th grade teacher wished to construct an assessment for the science measurement topic of *reproduction and heredity*. To construct Type I items for this topic, the teacher would ask and answer the following question: *About this measurement topic, what are the basic details and processes students should understand or be able to do fairly easily if they were paying attention in class?* For this particular topic, the teacher might decide that all students should be able to understand some basic terminology that was covered in class. She might devise some simple Type I items like the following:

Provide a brief explanation for each of the following terms:

1. heredity
2. offspring
3. sexual reproduction
4. asexual reproduction
5. gene

Although each of these terms represents very complex ideas, for these items the teacher wishes to determine only if students have a general understanding.

To construct Type II items for this topic, the teacher would ask and answer the following question: *About this measurement topic, what are the more complex ideas and processes students should understand and be able to do if they were paying attention in class?* Such knowledge might be more complex because it is broader in scope, less obvious, or has more component parts. For this particular topic, the teacher might construct the following item:

> Explain what would probably happen to a field of flowering plants if most of the insects and birds that visited the fields suddenly died and no other insects or birds replaced them.

The information addressed in this Type II item is considered more complex because it goes beyond the simple recall of characteristics of vocabulary terms. Rather, to answer the question, students must understand that flowering plants reproduce sexually, but they require insects and birds to transfer pollen from one flower to another. Thus, flowering plants are dependent on insects and birds for their survival. If the number of insects and birds servicing a given field dropped below a certain point, some of the plants would die. Such understanding is "generative" in nature in that it requires students to produce information— in this case, what might occur if the number of insects and birds decreased dramatically. To render this a Type II item, the teacher would have discussed with students the fact that flowering plants reproduce sexually without being in the same location, by relying on birds and insects to transport pollen. Thus, students who were attentive in class should be able to correctly answer the item even though the task demands more than recall of information.

To construct a Type III item, the teacher would ask and answer the following question: *About this measurement topic, what inferences and applications might students be able to make even though they go beyond what was taught in class?* For this particular topic, the teacher might construct the following task:

> Explain the differences between inherited traits and those that are caused by environment. Then list some traits you have that are inherited and some that are caused

by environment. Finally, explain why you think your behavior is affected more by your inherited traits or your environmental traits.

This Type III task has some features that are similar to the Type II task about flowering plants. Specifically, it also requires students to generate information. In this case, that information contains specific examples of inherited traits and environmental traits. The difference is that this task goes beyond the boundaries of what was taught in class; students are asked to apply their understanding of inherited and environmental traits to their own behavior. An important point is that this would not be a Type III task if the teacher previously had asked students to apply information presented in class to their behavior. A critical characteristic of a Type III task, then, is that it represents entirely new inferences and applications of content *not previously addressed in class*.

In summary, the design of Type I, II, and III items can be approached quite intuitively. A teacher simply asks and answers the following questions:

• About this measurement topic, what are the basic details and processes students should understand or be able to do fairly easily if they were paying attention in class?

• About this measurement topic, what are the more complex ideas and processes students should understand and be able to do if they were paying attention in class?

• About this measurement topic, what inferences and applications might students be able to make even though they go beyond what was taught in class?

Although the intuitive approach to designing Type I, II, and III items works well, a thorough understanding of different categories of knowledge allows for the design of even more effective items. Here we consider three categories of subject matter knowledge and the manner in which Type I, II, and III items or tasks manifest within each category. For a comprehensive discussion of these categories, see Marzano and Kendall (in press). The three categories of subject matter knowledge are (1) information, (2) mental procedures, and (3) psychomotor procedures.

Information

The first category of subject matter knowledge is *information*, more technically referred to as *declarative knowledge*. To illustrate, the following subject matter knowledge is informational in nature:

• Mathematics: Characteristics of proper and improper fractions
• Science: Bernoulli principle
• Language Arts: Characteristics of different types of genres

- Social Studies: Major events in the American Civil War
- Health and Physical Education: Defining features of addiction
- The Arts: Notes of the musical staff
- Technology: Parts of a computer
- Foreign Language: Vocabulary terms for familiar concepts

Type I Items and Tasks for Information

Information that is the focus of Type I items and tasks involves the basic details related to a measurement topic. Basic details take the form of vocabulary terms, facts, and time sequences (see Figure 4.2). The information is fairly straightforward from a learning perspective. It is not generative in nature, in that knowledge of details does not imply the production of new information. For example, knowing that the fictitious character Robin Hood first appeared in English literature in the early 1800s doesn't help a student generate new knowledge or imply that the student can do so.

Students typically demonstrate knowledge of details through recognition and recall items. For example, the following is a recognition item that a teacher might use to assess students' knowledge of details about the Battle of the Alamo:

Put an X next to the people who participated in the Battle of the Alamo:

_____ Sam Houston

_____ David "Davy" Crockett

_____ Jim Bowie

_____ Daniel Boone

_____ Lt. Col. William Barret Travis

_____ Capt. George Kimbell

_____ Col. James Fannin

_____ Kit Carson

Additionally, a teacher might use the following recall item to assess the same details:

Name the key individuals who participated in the Battle of the Alamo.

Type II Items and Tasks for Information

Information that is the focus of Type II items and tasks typically involves generalizations and principles (see Figure 4.3). By definition, generalizations and principles are more complex than details because they are generative in nature. Generalizations generate examples; principles generate predictions. In fact, to

---

FIGURE 4.2
Basic Details

Vocabulary terms are a common type of basic detail. Whether or not information qualifies as a vocabulary term is a function of how it is approached instructionally. For example, *heredity, offspring, sexual reproduction, asexual reproduction,* and *gene* all involve complex information, but each can be approached as a vocabulary term. When this is the case, the expectation is not that students can demonstrate in-depth knowledge, but rather that they have an accurate but somewhat surface-level understanding.

Facts are a type of informational knowledge that address details about specific persons, places, living things, nonliving things, events, and causes of specific events.

- *Characteristics of a specific real or fictional person:*
  - Neil Armstrong performed the first manned docking of two spacecraft in 1966 as part of the Gemini 8 mission and then was the first human to set foot on the moon in July 1969 as part of the Apollo II mission.
  - Charles Dickens wrote the book *David Copperfield* based in part on events in his own life.

- *Characteristics of a specific place:*
  - The elevation of Denver, Colorado, is 5,280 feet above sea level.

- *Characteristics of specific living things:*
  - The racehorse Seabiscuit inspired many people during the Great Depression because he was able to overcome injuries to become a champion.

- *Characteristics of specific nonliving things:*
  - The Rosetta Stone helped historians understand the origins of many passages in the Bible.

- *Characteristics of specific events:*
  - The attack on New York City on September 11, 2001, plunged the United States into a prolonged period of conflict.

- *Causes of specific events:*
  - The Boston Tea Party spurred the American colonists to defy British rule and proclaim the Declaration of Independence.

Time sequences involve events that occurred between two points in time. For example, the events that occurred between President Kennedy's assassination on November 22, 1963, and his burial on November 25 represent a time sequence.

---

demonstrate understanding of a generalization or a principle, a student must go beyond the ability to recall or recognize it; the student must be able to produce examples or predictions. For example, simply being able to repeat the Bernoulli principle does not mean a student understands the principle. Rather, understanding the Bernoulli principle involves being able to predict accurately what will happen in a given situation. A student who understands the Bernoulli principle can accurately predict which of two airplane wing designs will likely produce the most lift.

FIGURE 4.3
Generalizations and Principles

Generalizations are statements for which examples can be provided. A statement such as "Powerful leaders commonly arise during times of great crises" is a generalization. It is easy to confuse some types of generalizations with some types of facts. Facts identify characteristics of *specific* persons, places, living things, nonliving things, events, and causes of events, whereas generalizations identify characteristics of *classes* of the same types of information. For example, the information that taxation without representation was one of the causes of the Revolutionary War is factual. Information about causes of wars in general constitutes a generalization.

- *Characteristics of classes of real or fictional people*:
  - Early colonists had to endure many hardships.
  - Unicorn-like creatures are found in the mythologies of many cultures.

- *Characteristics of classes of places*:
  - Large cities have high crime rates.

- *Characteristics of classes of living things*:
  - Golden retrievers are good hunting dogs.

- *Characteristics of classes of nonliving things*:
  - Mountain ranges in various parts of the United States differ greatly in their altitudes and topographic characteristics.

- *Characteristics of classes of events*:
  - Earthquakes occur in a variety of intensities and a variety of durations.

- *Characteristics of classes of causal relationships*:
  - Acid rain is caused by a combination of unchecked industrial pollution and specific weather conditions.

- *Characteristics of abstractions*:
  - Duty is valued in most but not all societies.

Principles are a specific type of generalization that deals with cause/effect relationships. Like generalizations, principles are statements for which examples can be provided. However, principles are geared more toward predicting what will occur in a given situation. For example, the following statement is a principle: "The increase in lung cancer among women is directly proportional to the increase in the number of women who smoke." Once students understand the specifics of this principle, they can make specific predictions. For example, if they know the percentage increase of women who smoke in a specific setting, they could predict the percentage increase of women who will develop lung cancer.

Type II items and tasks for information are typically open ended in format. For example, the following is a Type II item a teacher might use to address the generalization that the cell membrane is selectively permeable.

In class we have found that the cell membrane is selectively permeable—it allows certain things to pass through but keeps out others. Provide specific examples of what the cell membrane will allow to pass through and what it will keep out. For each example, explain why it is allowed in or kept out.

Type III Items and Tasks for Information

As described previously, Type III items and tasks for information go beyond what was actually taught to students. By definition, inferences are required to correctly answer Type III items. However, Type II items also require inferences. For Type III items, though, the inferences and applications have not been addressed in class. One way to generate Type III informational items and tasks is to use one of the cognitive processes depicted in Figure 4.4. (For a more detailed description of the processes, see Marzano, 2004b.) For example, a teacher who has presented information about meiosis and mitosis might create a comparing task by asking students to describe how the two processes are similar and different.

A classifying task is easily generated if a set of related information has been presented to students. For example, assume that an art teacher has taught information about the following: overlapping, adding in sculpture, shading, subtracting, varying size, varying color, mixing color, and perspective. To generate a Type III task, the teacher might ask students to organize the list into two or more categories. Students also would be asked to explain the rules for category membership and defend why each item was placed in its respective category.

Creating metaphors involves making connections between information that does not appear related on the surface. An example of a metaphor is "Love is a rose." On the surface, love and a rose do not appear related. At an abstract level,

---

FIGURE 4.4
Cognitive Processes Used in Type III Informational Items and Tasks

Comparing is the process of identifying similarities and differences among or between things or ideas. Technically speaking, *comparing* refers to identifying similarities, and *contrasting* refers to identifying differences. However, many educators use the term *comparing* to refer to both.

Classifying is the process of grouping things that are alike into categories based on their characteristics.

Creating metaphors is the process of identifying a general or basic pattern that connects information that is not related at the surface or literal level.

Creating analogies is the process of identifying the relationship between two sets of items—in other words, identifying the relationship between relationships.

Analyzing errors is the process of identifying and correcting errors in the way information is presented or applied.

however, it is possible to discern linkages. Both are alluring, and both can result in pain. To construct a Type III task that involves creating metaphors, a teacher might ask students to describe similarities between two elements that do not appear related on the surface. Asking students to explain how the cell is like a factory would be an example of a metaphor task.

Creating analogies involves identifying relationships between relationships. Analogies have the form "A is to B as C is to D." The following are analogy tasks that a science teacher might generate:

Explain each of the following:

- Oxygen is to humans as carbon dioxide is to plants.
- Nucleus is to atom as core is to the Earth.
- Newton is to force and motion as Bernoulli is to air pressure.

Alternatively, a Type III task might require students to generate their own analogies as opposed to explaining those provided by the teacher.

Analyzing errors involves identifying and explaining what is incorrect about information. To illustrate, assume that a teacher had presented information about the sun and its relationship to the Earth. She might generate an error-analysis task such as the following:

Sally knows that she is most likely to get a sunburn if she is out in the sun between 11:00 a.m. and 1:00 p.m. She asks six of her friends why this is so. Identify which answers are wrong and explain the error made in each:

- Answer #1: We are slightly closer to the sun at noon than in the morning or afternoon.
- Answer #2: More "burn" will be produced by the noon sun than the morning or afternoon sun.
- Answer #3: When the sun's rays fall straight down (directly) on a surface, more energy is received than when they fall indirectly on the surface.
- Answer #4: When the sun is directly overhead, its rays pass through less atmosphere than when it is lower in the sky.
- Answer #5: The air is usually warmer at noon than at any other time of the day.
- Answer #6: The ultraviolet rays of sunlight are mainly responsible for sunburn. They are most intense during these hours.

In summary, Type I items and tasks for information focus on basic details such as vocabulary terms, facts, and time sequences. Type II items and tasks focus on generalizations and principles. Type III items and tasks require inferences and applications that go beyond what was presented in class. Type III items and tasks sometimes involve cognitive operations of comparing, classifying, creating metaphors, creating analogies, and analyzing errors.

Mental Procedures

The second category of subject matter content is mental procedures. In technical terms, mental procedures are a type of procedural knowledge as opposed to declarative knowledge or information. About the declarative vs. procedural distinction, psychologists Robert Snow and David Lohman (1989) note, "The distinction between declarative knowledge and procedural knowledge, or more simply content knowledge and process knowledge" is one of the most basic in terms of guiding educational practice (p. 266). Psychologist John Anderson (1983) has described the basic structure of procedural knowledge in terms of "IF-THEN" structures referred to as "production networks." The following example (Marzano, 2001) shows a small part of a production network for the mental procedure of multicolumn subtraction:

> 1a. IF the goal is to do multicolumn subtraction,
> 1b. THEN process the rightmost column.
> 2a. IF an answer has been recorded in the current column and there is a column to the left,
> 2b. THEN process the column to the left.
> 3a. IF the goal is to process the column and there is no bottom digit or the bottom digit is zero,
> 3b. THEN record the top digit as the answer, and so on. (p. 24)

Production networks like this one are used by artificial-intelligence scientists to program computers to behave in ways that simulate human thought. They are not designed as instructional tools. However, the example does demonstrate the basic nature of a mental procedure. It is a series of steps that result in a product. In this case, the product is the answer to a multicolumn subtraction problem.

At first glance, some educators might react negatively to this way of looking at mental procedures because it seems to imply that there is only one way to carry out a procedure, and that procedures should be taught in a lockstep, didactic fashion. In fact, this is not the case. Psychologists inform us that learning a mental (or psychomotor) procedure involves a series of stages. The first is referred to as the "cognitive" stage (Fitts & Posner, 1967). At this stage, learners can't actually perform the procedure in any effective way, but they do have a general understanding of the steps. A teacher may have presented these steps to the students, or the students might have constructed the steps on their own via trial and error. Both approaches are legitimate, although some cognitive psychologists believe that educators have an unfortunate bias that favors the discovery approach over demonstrating or presenting students with the steps (see Anderson, Greeno, Reder, & Simon, 2000; Anderson, Reder, & Simon, 1995, 1996).

Regardless of how students obtain their initial understanding of the steps involved in a procedure, the steps are changed and amended in the next stage of learning, the "associative" stage. At this stage, errors in the initial steps are identified, deleted, and replaced by more effective steps. Even if a set of steps is not flawed, learners might replace it with a set that is more consistent with their background knowledge or that they prefer stylistically. During the third stage, the "autonomous" stage, the procedure is refined to a point at which it can be executed with little or minimal conscious thought (LaBerge & Samuels, 1974).

Type I Items and Tasks for Mental Procedures

Type I items and tasks for mental procedures typically focus on procedures with fairly straightforward steps that generate a product with little or no variation. For example, the mental procedure for performing multicolumn subtraction, when executed correctly, results in a single correct answer. Mental procedures that are the focus of Type I items and tasks include single rules, algorithms, and tactics (see Figure 4.5).

Often the single rule, algorithm, or tactic that is the focus of a Type I item is a component of a more robust and more complex procedure (discussed in the next section on Type II items and tasks for mental procedures). For example, the mental procedure of using single rules for capitalization is embedded in the more robust procedure of editing for mechanics.

Type I items and tasks for mental procedures frequently take the form of exercises (see Frisbie, 2005) that require students to execute the mental procedure in a highly structured situation. For example, the following are some Type I items a

---

FIGURE 4.5
Mental Procedures for Type I Items and Tasks

Single rules or a small set of rules constitute the simplest type of mental procedure. For example, rules for capitalization are single-rule mental procedures: IF the word begins a sentence, THEN capitalize the word.

Algorithms are mental procedures that do not vary much in their application once learned. Multicolumn addition and subtraction are examples of algorithms. Once students have learned the steps to the level of automaticity, they usually execute the steps the same way.

Tactics exhibit more variation in their execution than do single rules or algorithms in that a person might use a tactic differently from one situation to another. For example, a person might vary the process used to read a map depending on the situation and the type of map.

mathematics teacher might use to assess students' abilities to perform the mental procedure of multicolumn multiplication using whole numbers:

$32 \times 15 =$

$17 \times 47 =$

$132 \times 25 =$

$99 \times 14 =$

$121 \times 134 =$

Type II Items and Tasks for Mental Procedures

Type II items and tasks typically address more complex mental procedures technically referred to as *macroprocedures* (see Marzano & Kendall, 1996). They are complex in the sense that they involve embedded procedures. For example, the macroprocedure of writing involves embedded procedures for gathering information, organizing ideas, developing an initial draft, revising, editing, and publishing. Additionally, the procedures embedded within a macroprocedure will commonly involve embedded elements. For example, the subcomponent of editing involves embedded components such as editing for overall logic, editing for grammar, and editing for conventions. Finally, macroprocedures are also characterized by the fact that they produce multiple viable products. For example, two students writing on the same topic might produce very different compositions, both of which demonstrate sound use of the writing process.

Macroprocedures are not as numerous as single rules, algorithms, and tactics. In addition to writing, reading qualifies as a macroprocedure, as do using a word processor, using the Internet, conducting a musical piece, preparing a meal, planning an event, debating, using a complex mathematical calculator, staging a musical, and so on. Figure 4.6 presents a popular and important set of general macroprocedures.

The macroprocedures in Figure 4.6 are sometimes embedded in specific subject areas. For example, problem solving is addressed in mathematics, experimental inquiry in science, decision making in social studies, and so on. However, these procedures are cross-curricular in that they can be addressed in multiple subject areas. For example, problem solving might be addressed in technology classes, and decision making might be addressed in health and physical education.

Type II items for mental procedures are typically more open ended than are Type I items. For example, here is a problem-solving task a theater teacher might present to students:

FIGURE 4.6
General Macroprocedures

Decision making is the process of generating and applying criteria to select from among seemingly equal alternatives.

Problem solving is the process of overcoming constraints or limiting conditions that are in the way of pursuing goals.

Experimental inquiry is the process of generating and testing explanations of observed phenomena.

Investigation is the process of identifying and resolving issues that involve confusions or contradictions.

Invention is the process of developing unique products or processes that fulfill perceived needs.

You are putting on the play *Our Town* but have no money to build a set. In fact, you can use only boxes as your staging materials. Draw a sketch of how you would stage a particular scene, and explain how your use of the boxes is called for by the scene.

Type III Items and Tasks for Mental Procedures

Type III items for mental procedures address the extent to which students can apply the procedure in a context not addressed in class. For example, assume that a teacher had taught multicolumn subtraction in the context of the following format:

375
−291

To design a Type III task for this mental procedure, the teacher might simply change the format and context in which students are presented with the basic information for the procedure. That new format might be a word problem like this:

You are saving money to buy a new bicycle that costs 375 dollars. You have already saved 291 dollars. How much more do you need to save?

What would make this a Type III task is not a characteristic of the task itself, but rather whether the task is new to students. As before, Type III items and tasks for mental procedures require students to provide new applications that have not been directly addressed in class. Consequently, if the teacher had presented students with multicolumn subtraction word problems in class, then the example would not be a Type III task. To provide another example, assume a teacher wished to design a Type III task for the mental procedure of editing a composition for overall logic. If the teacher had taught and reinforced the procedure using short stories, a Type III task for the procedure might be to use it with a poem.

This discussion of Type III items for mental procedures and the previous discussion of Type III items for information help clarify the values of 4.0 and 3.5 on the complete scale presented in Chapter 3. Recall that a score of 4.0 is assigned when the student demonstrates *inferences* and *applications* that go beyond what was taught in class. *Inferences* involve information; *applications* involve mental and psychomotor procedures (discussed in the next section). For both inferences and applications, the critical characteristic that would justify a score of 4.0 is that new environments and situations are involved that have not been addressed explicitly in class. Thus a score of 4.0 indicates that a student has exceeded the curriculum addressed in class. Recall from the score distribution depicted in Figure 3.7 that only a small proportion of students will typically demonstrate this level of competence. A scale should be sensitive to this advanced level of performance. In fact, the term *advanced* (used by many districts to describe one level of performance) typically means "ahead or further ahead in progress." A score of 3.5 also indicates that a student goes beyond what was explicitly addressed in class, although the student's inferences and applications are only partially accurate.

Psychomotor Procedures

As the name implies, psychomotor procedures involve physical procedures individuals use to engage in physical activities for work or for recreation. Examples of psychomotor procedures include playing defense in basketball, hitting a baseball, performing a folk dance, singing an aria from an opera, performing a scene from a play, and driving in city traffic.

Like mental procedures, psychomotor procedures are stored as IF/THEN structures or production networks. Also, the stages of learning a psychomotor procedure are similar to those for learning a mental procedure (see Anderson, 1983, 1995; Gagne, 1977, 1989). Specifically, during the first stage (the cognitive stage), the student develops an understanding of the steps involved but cannot actually perform them. During the second stage (the associative stage), the student adds to and alters the initial set of steps presented or discovered, making the set more effective and personally comfortable. During the third stage (the autonomous stage), the student practices and refines the procedure so that it can be performed with relative ease.

Type I Items and Tasks for Psychomotor Procedures

Like Type I items for mental procedures, Type I items for psychomotor procedures frequently focus on the pieces or component parts of a more robust psychomotor procedure. For example, within the robust procedure of playing defense in basketball, a physical education teacher might wish to focus on the component psychomotor skill of quick lateral movement while keeping one's body between the basket and the player being guarded. Similarly, within the robust psychomotor procedure of driving in city traffic, a driver's education teacher might wish to focus on parallel parking.

Type I tasks for psychomotor procedures do not lend themselves to paper-and-pencil assessments. Rather they are most effectively assessed using some form of physical demonstration or performance. Obviously a student must physically execute a psychomotor procedure to demonstrate competence. To assess the psychomotor procedure of lateral movement while playing defense, the physical education teacher would have students guard an offensive player trying to score a goal. To assess the psychomotor procedure of parallel parking, the driver's education teacher would have students parallel park a car.

Type II Items and Tasks for Psychomotor Procedures

Type II items and tasks for psychomotor procedures typically address complex procedures that usually consist of many subcomponents. As described earlier, the subcomponent psychomotor procedure of moving laterally in an appropriate defensive position is embedded in the more robust psychomotor procedure of playing defense in basketball. The subcomponent psychomotor procedure of parallel parking is embedded in the more robust procedure of driving in city traffic. Again, Type II tasks rely on demonstration. In the case of the procedure for playing defense, students would be assessed by having them take part in a basketball scrimmage. In the case of driving in city traffic, students would be assessed by actually driving in the city.

Type III Items and Tasks for Psychomotor Procedures

Type III items for psychomotor procedures address the extent to which students perform a psychomotor procedure in a situation not directly addressed in class. For example, if playing defense against one particular type of offense was the focus of a Type II task, playing defense against a type of offense not directly addressed in class would constitute a Type III task. A Type III task for parallel parking would be parallel parking in a space that is inordinately small or on a steep incline, assuming that these situations had not been previously encountered.

Item and Task Types

The discussion thus far implies that different types of items and tasks are required for different types of knowledge. That is, the types of items and tasks that are most useful when assessing information are different from the types of items and tasks that are most useful when assessing mental procedures or psychomotor procedures. In this section we consider common item and task formats and their relationships to information, mental procedures, and psychomotor procedures. We consider five categories of items and tasks: forced-choice, short written response, essays, oral responses and reports, and demonstrations and performances.

Forced-Choice Items and Tasks

Forced-choice items and tasks are a staple of educational assessment. As described in Chapter 3, the testing movement of the early 20th century relied on items that could be scored as correct or incorrect. Such is the nature of forced-choice items.

In general, forced-choice items can be organized into six categories (see Figure 4.7). Forced-choice items are quite useful and appropriate for information, particularly for vocabulary terms, facts, and time sequences. As such, forced-choice items and tasks are frequently used in Type I situations. In Figure 4.7, the example for the traditional multiple-choice format addresses the vocabulary term *region,* and the fill-in-the-blank example addresses the term *selectively permeable.* Facts are the focus of the two multiple-response examples in Figure 4.7. As illustrated in the first example for matching items, forced-choice items can also be used for mental procedures. In this case, students must perform a specific computational procedure before they can select the correct answer.

Short Written Response

By definition, a short written response is a type of "constructed-response" item or task as opposed to a forced-choice item or task. As the name implies, constructed-response items and tasks require students to construct a correct answer as opposed to recognizing one. To illustrate, the following is a short written response task that might be used in an economics class:

> Explain how a dramatic increase in gasoline prices is an example of the principle of supply and demand.

To answer this item, students must retrieve information about supply and demand, organize the information in a logical manner, and then explain their logic. As this example illustrates, short constructed-response items and tasks are

FIGURE 4.7
Types of Forced-Choice Items

1. **Traditional Multiple-Choice**—Provides a stem and alternatives, some of which are distractors and one of which is the correct choice.

   (Stem) The best definition of a *region* is . . .

   A. An area of land between two bodies of water (distractor)
   B. An area of land that has common topographical or political features (correct choice)
   C. An area of land that is a specific size (distractor)
   D. An area of land that has a specific shape (distractor)

2. **Matching**—Provides multiple stems and multiple options.

   Traditional format

(Stems)			(Options)			
A. 3×5	=	_____	1. 28		6. 15	
B. $7 / 6$	=	_____	2. 1.05		7. 1.28	
C. 12×13	=	_____	3. 120		8. 114	
D. 7×6	=	_____	4. 156		9. 42	
			5. 22		10. 1.17	

   Expanded format

Person	Activity	Time
A. Kennedy	1. Led U.S. forces in Europe (WWII)	6. About 1790
B. Jefferson	2. Was elected first Roman Catholic president	7. About 1980
C. Reagan	3. Was elected first U.S. president	8. About 1800
	4. Purchased Louisiana Territory	9. About 1860
	5. Hostages released at start of presidency	10. About 1960

3. **Alternative Choice**—Provides a stem and two choices that are quite similar.

   Traditional format

   (Stem) The part of speech used to link two clauses is . . .

   A. a preposition
   B. a conjunction

   Alternative format

   (A. An architect, B. A draftsman) is an engineer who designs buildings.

4. **True/False**—Provides statements that must be judged as true or false.

   Mark F if the statement is false and T if the statement is true.

   _____ 1. The first thing to do with an automobile that does not start is to check the battery.

   _____ 2. A cause of premature tire wear is improper tire pressure.

FIGURE 4.7

Types of Forced-Choice Items *(continued)*

_____ 3. The automobile's onboard computer should be replaced if the automobile drives poorly.

_____ 4. Under harsh driving conditions, an automobile's oil should be changed every 3 months/3,000 miles, whichever comes first.

5. Fill-in-the-Blank—Provides a stem for which only one correct response is reasonable.

As it relates to the cell membrane, the term *selectively permeable* means that it allows in _____, but keeps out _____.

6. Multiple-Response—Allows for two or more correct responses.

Traditional format

Which of the following can be the end punctuation for a sentence?

1. A period
2. A dash
3. An exclamation point
4. A question mark

A. 1 and 2
B. 2, 3, and 4
C. 1, 3, and 4
D. 2 and 3

Alternative format

Place a Y in front of each event listed below that occurred at the Battle of Gettysburg.

_____ 1. Pickett's Charge

_____ 2. the end of the Civil War

_____ 3. Confederate soldiers occupied Culps Hill

_____ 4. Meade's Maneuver

_____ 5. 15 citizens of Gettysburg killed at Devil's Den

---

frequently used in Type II situations involving information. The item in this example requires students to demonstrate an understanding of a specific principle.

Short written responses are also useful formats for designing Type III tasks for information. Recall that Type III tasks for information frequently require students to compare, classify, create metaphors, create analogies, or analyze errors. All of these are easily framed as a short written response. To illustrate, the following is a short written response Type III task involving the principle of supply and demand:

Compare the principle of supply and demand with the principle of overproduction. Describe specific ways in which they are similar and specific ways in which they are different. Then describe one or more conclusions your analysis leads you to and defend those conclusions.

Short written responses are also quite useful as Type I, Type II, and Type III tasks for mental procedures. To illustrate, consider the mental procedure of reading a map of the city. Students might be presented with the map and a series of Type I short written response items such as the following:

1. Describe what each symbol in the map legend tells you.

2. Put a circle around the downtown mall and describe the quadrant of the map it is in and where it is within that quadrant.

3. Identify which of the following are farthest away from each other: the mall, the baseball stadium, the factory. Explain how you computed the various distances.

4. Describe the shortest route from the baseball stadium to the mall using one-way streets only.

Short written responses are also useful for designing Type II items and tasks for mental procedures. To illustrate, consider the following set of short written response items that might be used to assess the mental procedure of experimental inquiry:

In class, we discussed the idea that some people believe that weather and climate affect people's moods and personalities.

1. Describe something you have noticed about the relationship between weather/climate and mood/personality.

2. Make a prediction based on what you have noticed regarding this relationship.

3. Explain how you might set up an experiment to test your prediction.

4. Explain what type of outcome you would need to show that your prediction was accurate.

Finally, short written responses also can be used to construct Type III items and tasks for mental procedures. To illustrate, consider this Type III item for the mental procedure of reading the city map mentioned earlier:

Pretend that you were going to redesign the city map you have been given. Explain the changes you would make to the map legend as well as to the map itself. For each change, explain why it would improve the current version of the map.

Essays

According to Mark Durm (1993), essays were one of the first forms of assessment used in public education. Essays and short written responses obviously are similar in that students must construct responses in written form. However, essays typically provide students with more structure than do short written responses, and they allow for more coverage of a given measurement topic. To illustrate, consider the following essay task:

> In 1858, Abraham Lincoln and Stephen Douglas debated during the campaign for the Senate seat representing the state of Illinois. You've been provided with a portion of what each of the debaters said. Read the comments of both Douglas and Lincoln and then respond to each of the following questions:
>
> 1. Douglas referred to a speech made by Lincoln in Springfield. What speech was Douglas referring to?
> 2. What did Douglas mean by the statement "The Republic has existed from 1789 to this day divided into Free States and Slave States"?
> 3. In class we have talked about the generalization that for every defensible proposal, there is a defensible counterproposal. Explain how the Lincoln–Douglas debate exemplifies this generalization.
> 4. Identify a modern-day situation that reminds you of the Lincoln–Douglas debate. Explain how the debate and this situation are similar and different.

Essays frequently provide students with information to react to. Along with this essay task, students would be provided with the excerpts from the Lincoln–Douglas debate shown in Figure 4.8.

A useful aspect of essays is that they can be designed to include Type I, Type II, and Type III elements all within the same essay. Questions 1 and 2 in the example are Type I in nature in that they deal with factual information. Question 3 is Type II in nature in that it addresses a generalization. Question 4 is Type III in nature in that it requires students to go beyond what was presented in class.

As the Lincoln–Douglas task illustrates, essays are useful for assessing informational knowledge. One might argue that, like short written responses, essays are also useful for assessing mental procedures. This might be true; however, essays require a fairly sophisticated level of writing ability. Indeed, one common reason for using essays is to assess writing ability. Given that short written responses adequately address mental procedures and are not as dependent on writing ability, it is advisable to rely on them (as opposed to essays) to assess mental procedures.

Oral Responses and Oral Reports

In one sense, oral responses and reports can be thought of as short written responses or essays in oral form. In fact, the essay example about the Lincoln–Douglas debate could easily be translated into an oral report simply by requiring students to present their answers orally. If the emphasis is on students' demonstration of knowledge as opposed to their ability to make presentations, then oral responses and reports are similar to short written responses. Thus, they are good vehicles for Type I, II, and III tasks involving information as well as mental procedures. In fact, each example provided in the discussion of short written response could easily be transformed into an oral response or report.

One form of oral response that is probably underused for classroom assessment is impromptu discussions between the teacher and students. Specifically, as time and circumstances allow, the teacher simply asks specific students to discuss

---

FIGURE 4.8
Excerpts from the Lincoln–Douglas Debate

Stephen A. Douglas

Mr. Lincoln tells you, in his speech made at Springfield, before the Convention which gave him his unanimous nomination, that—

"A house divided against itself cannot stand."
"I believe this government cannot endure permanently, half slave and half free."
"I do not expect the Union to be dissolved, I don't expect the house to fall; but I do expect it will cease to be divided."
"It will become all one thing or all the other."

That is the fundamental principle upon which he sets out in this campaign. Well, I do not suppose you will believe one word of it when you come to examine it carefully, and see its consequences. Although the Republic has existed from 1789 to this day, divided into Free States and Slave States, yet we are told that in the future it cannot endure unless they shall become all free or all slave. For that reason he says . . . .

Abraham Lincoln

Judge Douglas made two points upon my recent speech at Springfield. He says they are to be the issues of this campaign. The first one of these points he bases upon the language in a speech which I delivered at Springfield which I believe I can quote correctly from memory. I said there that "we are now far into the fifth year since a policy was instituted for the avowed object, and with the confident purpose, of putting an end to slavery agitation; under the operation of that policy, that agitation had not only not ceased, but had constantly augmented." "I believe it will not cease until a crisis shall have been reached and passed. 'A house divided against itself cannot stand.' I believe this Government cannot endure permanently, half slave and half free." "I do not expect the Union to be dissolved"—I am quoting from my speech—"I do not expect the house to fall, but I do expect it will cease to be divided. It will become one thing or the other. Either the opponents of slavery will arrest the spread of it and place it where the public mind shall rest, in the belief that it is in the course of ultimate extinction, or its advocates will push it forward until it shall become alike lawful in all the States, North as well as South. . . .

Source: From *Political Debates Between Abraham Lincoln and Stephen A. Douglas,* by Cleveland (1902) in Baker, Aschbacher, Niemi, and Sato (1992, pp. 43–47).

a particular measurement topic. For example, as the teacher walks around the room while students are doing seatwork, a student might ask the teacher a question. Sensing that the student is grappling with a particular topic, the teacher would initiate a discussion.

This form of interaction is potentially one of the most useful forms of classroom assessment. To illustrate, researcher Sheila Valencia and her colleagues conducted a study of 44 elementary students and 31 junior high school students (Valencia, Stallman, Commeyras, Pearson, & Hartman, 1991). They assessed each student's knowledge of specific topics in four ways: a structured discussion, a fill-in-the blank test, a short-answer test, and an essay. In structured discussion, the teacher simply asked a specific student questions regarding knowledge of the topic, and the student responded orally. The structured discussion provided more information by far than any of the other three types of assessments. Specifically, the other three types provided only 34 percent of the information that was provided by the structured discussion. As the researchers note: "On average, 66 percent of the typically relevant ideas students gave during the interviews were not tested on any of the . . . [other] measures" (p. 226). One of Valencia's final conclusions is that "a comprehensive view of a person's topical knowledge may well require multiple measures, each of which contributes unique information to the picture" (p. 230).

Demonstrations and Performances

As their names imply, demonstrations and performances require students to "do something." Stated in technical terms, demonstrations and performances require students to execute a procedure. As such, they are perfect vehicles for Type I, II, and III tasks involving psychomotor procedures. To illustrate, a Type I task for guarding a basketball player in a one-on-one situation is simply asking students to execute the process. A Type II task for playing defense in a five-on-five situation is asking students to demonstrate their competence during a game. A Type III task for playing defense in basketball is asking students to execute the defense against a type of offense that was not addressed in class. In short, demonstrations and performances are the natural way to assess psychomotor procedures.

Matching Item Types to Kinds of Knowledge

Each of the five types of classroom assessment—forced-choice items, short written response, essays, oral responses and reports, and demonstrations and performances—is suitable for assessing certain kinds of knowledge. Figure 4.9 shows

	Forced Choice	Short Written Response	Essay	Oral Responses & Reports	Demonstrations & Performances
FIGURE 4.9					
Kinds of Knowledge, Types of Items and Tasks, and Forms of Assessment					
Information					
Type I	X	X	X	X	
Type II		X	X	X	
Type III		X	X	X	
Mental Procedures					
Type I	X	X		X	
Type II		X		X	
Type III		X		X	
Psychomotor Procedures					
Type I					X
Type II					X
Type III					X

the relationship between these various forms of assessment, kinds of knowledge, and types of tasks.

Revisiting the Design and Scoring of Classroom Assessments

An intuitive approach to designing classroom assessments was presented at the beginning of this chapter. As viable as that approach is, a firm grounding in the three types of knowledge—information, mental procedures, and psychomotor procedures—and their relationship to Type I, II, and III items provides teachers with many options when designing classroom assessments, as well as a better understanding of the assessments that are designed. To illustrate, let's reconsider the assessment on the topic of reproduction and heredity presented at the beginning of the chapter in the context of the intuitive approach to assessment design. In retrospect we see that the content was informational in nature. We also recognize that the assessment relied exclusively on short written responses. Armed with a thorough knowledge of the item formats discussed earlier, the teacher might decide to use matching items like the following for the Type I tasks:

> Match each vocabulary term with the answer that best describes it by writing the letter of the correct answer next to its corresponding vocabulary term. There are more answers than there are vocabulary terms, so you won't find a term for every answer.

Vocabulary term	Answer
• heredity	(a) the process that results in an offspring that is an exact copy of the one parent
• offspring	
• sexual reproduction	(b) the product of the reproductive process of an animal or plant
• asexual reproduction	
• gene	(c) the process of passing instructions for specifying traits from one generation to another
	(d) the process that involves a male and female parent
	(e) the product of asexual reproduction
	(f) the element of a cell that carries a single unit of information
	(g) the product of a cell dividing
	(h) the element of a cell that allows the cell to split
	(i) the contribution of the male in the reproductive process
	(j) the part of the cell that houses the chromosomes
	(k) the type of reproduction used by all animals and all forms of bacteria

For the Type II items the teacher might decide to use a combination of a traditional multiple-choice item and a short written response item:

Which of the following best explains what would happen to a field of flowering plants if most of the insects and birds that visited the field suddenly died out and no other insects or birds replaced them? When you have selected your answer, explain what is incorrect about each of the answers you did not select.

(a) The plants would all die out because the birds and insects leave fertilizer that makes the plants grow.

(b) The plants wouldn't be affected too much because they can live without birds and insects.

(c) The plants would all die because insects and birds help the plants reproduce sexually.

(d) The plants would all die because the insects and birds help the plants reproduce asexually.

(e) Some but not all of the plants would die because the insects and birds help the plants reproduce sexually.

(f) Some but not all of the plants would die because the insects and birds help the plants reproduce asexually.

Finally, for the Type III item the teacher might decide to use the short written response format presented previously:

Explain the differences between inherited traits and those that are caused by environment. Then list some traits you have that are inherited and some that are caused by environment. Finally, explain why you think your behavior is affected more by your inherited traits or your environmental traits.

As described in Chapter 3, to score the assessment the teacher would mark each item as receiving full credit (+), no credit (0), or partial credit (*part*). Examining each student's pattern of responses across the three types of items, the teacher would assign the most appropriate score.

Revisiting the Issue of Illogical Response Patterns

As mentioned in Chapter 3, sometimes students' response patterns will not seem logical. For example, assume that a student missed a specific forced-choice Type I item but correctly answered all Type II items. One possible reason for an aberrant response pattern is that a particular item does not address Type I knowledge—the easier information, mental procedures, or psychomotor procedures. It is important to remember that a specific piece of information, mental procedure, or psychomotor procedure is not easy or difficult in itself even though it is true that some knowledge is more complex than other knowledge (e.g., a generalization is more complex than a fact; a macroprocedure is more complex than a procedure). Rather, the extent to which knowledge has been explicitly addressed in class has a strong bearing on whether it is easy or difficult for students. A majority of students incorrectly responding to an item is a good sign that the knowledge involved was not addressed adequately in class. To compensate, the teacher need only reclassify the item as Type II.

Another possibility is that a particular student was simply careless when responding to an item or misunderstood its intent. The best way to address this is to return the assessment to the student with a written (or oral) comment such as this: "If you had answered item 5 correctly, I could have given you a 3.0. Instead I scored your test a 1.5 because missing item 5 indicates that you are having difficulty with some basic facts." Additionally, the teacher could invite the student to demonstrate that he understands the basic information represented in the item by, for example, completing some Type I exercises in the textbook, or exercises that the teacher provides, or some that the student designs on his own. In each case, the student is given the responsibility and the opportunity to demonstrate that his incorrect responses on the easier items were anomalies. This is not only sound assessment practice but also sound instructional practice.

The example just presented involves written responses. Now let's consider an assessment that uses a performance or demonstration. Again, the example involves playing defense in basketball. As students perform, the physical education teacher observes each individual. The teacher first observes how students perform the Type I component skills and records that score for each student. As with other types of assessments, the teacher uses the symbols +, 0, or *part*, representing the student's performance on the component skills. Next the teacher observes the student's overall defensive play, scoring the student in a similar fashion. If a particular student demonstrated competence in the more complex psychomotor procedures (e.g., overall defensive play) but exhibited errors in the component skill of proper body position, the teacher might invite the student to address this anomaly by demonstrating proper form after the scrimmage.

Assessing the Life Skill Topics

Chapter 2 addressed the importance of life skill topics such as class participation, work completion, behavior, and teamwork. These also should be assessed throughout a grading period. To do so requires a scale designed for each life skill topic that the district or school has identified. Figure 4.10 shows general scales for the life skill topics *participation*, *work completion*, *behavior*, and *working in groups*. One thing to note about the general scales in Figure 4.10 is that they are, in fact, very general. As discussed in Chapter 2, a district or school should identify specific behaviors for specific grade levels for each life skill topic. For example, for *participation* at the middle school level, a district or school might identify the following behaviors:

- Making an attempt to answer questions asked by the teacher
- Volunteering ideas without being called on
- Paying attention to presentations

These behaviors would be written into each scale. For example, for a score value of 3.0, the *participation* scale might include the following component:

> The student's classroom participation meets identified expectations including
>
> - Making an attempt to answer questions asked by the teacher
> - Volunteering ideas without being called on
> - Paying attention to presentations

Another thing to note about the general scales is that they involve whole-point values only. As discussed in Chapter 3, for some measurement topics the simplified scale seems more appropriate than the complete scale. Life skill topics generally are more amenable to the simplified scale than the complete scale.

Unlike academic measurement topics, life skill topics are assessed via teacher observation. Audrey Kleinsasser (1991) explains that teacher observation involves the "informal conversations with students and observations of students that teachers make all day" (p. 9). Rick Stiggins (1994) provides the following example of a teacher observing a student's social skills:

	FIGURE 4.10 General Scoring Scales for Life Skill Topics			
	Participation	**Work Completion**	**Behavior**	**Working in Groups**
4.0	In addition to level 3.0 performance, the student participates in ways not explicitly expected in class.	In addition to level 3.0 performance, the student goes beyond the required conventions.	In addition to level 3.0 performance, the student follows rules and procedures that have not been specifically required.	In addition to level 3.0 performance, the student exhibits group maintenance and interpersonal skills that have not been explicitly identified.
3.0	The student's participation meets classroom expectations.	The student hands in work on time and meets all required conventions.	The student's behavior follows all classroom rules and procedures.	In groups, the student exhibits group maintenance and interpersonal skills that have been identified.
2.0	With some noteworthy exceptions, the student's participation meets classroom expectations.	With some noteworthy exceptions, the student hands in work on time and meets required conventions.	With some noteworthy exceptions, the student's behavior follows classroom rules and procedures.	With some noteworthy exceptions, the student exhibits group maintenance and interpersonal skills that have been identified.
1.0	With help or prodding, the student's participation meets classroom expectations.	With help or prodding, the student hands in work on time and meets required conventions.	With help or prodding, the student's behavior follows classroom rules and procedures.	With help or prodding, the student exhibits group maintenance and interpersonal skills that have been identified.
0.0	Even with help or prodding, the student's participation does not meet classroom expectations.	Even with help or prodding, the student does not hand in work on time or meet required conventions.	Even with help or prodding, the student's behavior does not follow classroom rules and procedures.	Even with help or prodding, the student does not exhibit group maintenance and interpersonal skills that have been identified.

For example, a primary grade teacher might watch a student interacting with classmates and draw inferences about that child's level of development in social interaction skills. If the levels of achievement are clearly defined in terms the observer can easily interpret, then the teacher, observing carefully, can derive information from watching that will aid in planning strategies to promote further social development.

Thus, this is not an assessment where answers are counted right or wrong. Rather, like the essay test, we rely on teacher judgment to place the student's performance somewhere on a continuum of achievement levels ranging from very low to very high. (p. 160)

One option for observing the life skill topics is to select a specific day each week when scores for the life skills are assigned to students. For example, a high school social studies teacher might use the last 10 minutes of class each Friday to assign scores to each student regarding performance that week on *class participation*, *work completion*, *behavior*, and *teamwork*. Thus, over a nine-week grading period, the teacher would have recorded nine scores on all of the life skill topics for each student.

An interesting variation on this theme is to ask students to score themselves on the life skill topics at the same time. The students' self-assigned scores might be compared with those assigned by the teacher. Any discrepancies might be the subject of discussion between the teacher and the students. Another option is to record scores for students on the life skills as they are observed. For example, if the teacher notices that a given student is working in a group particularly well on a given day, the teacher might record a score for that one student only for the life skill *working in groups*. This "situational score" can be added to the scores that are recorded every Friday at the end of class.

Summary and Conclusions

Knowledge can be divided into three types: information, mental procedures, and psychomotor procedures. Assessment items and tasks can be grouped into three categories: Type I, which address basic details and skills; Type II, which address more complex ideas and processes; and Type III, which require students to make inferences or applications that go beyond what was taught in class. Assessment items can be designed in five formats: forced-choice, short written response, essays, oral reports and responses, and demonstrations and performances. Classroom teachers have a wide range of options when designing formative classroom assessments.

5

Assessments That Encourage Learning

Of the four principles of effective classroom assessment discussed in Chapter 1, the second principle—that it should encourage students to improve—is probably the most challenging to implement. As we saw in Chapter 1, feedback can have varying effects on student learning. If done the wrong way, it can discourage learning. Figure 1.2 in Chapter 1 illustrates that simply telling students their answers are right or wrong has a negative influence on student learning. The positive effects of feedback are not automatic. This chapter presents three techniques that encourage learning.

Tracking Students' Progress

One of the most powerful and straightforward ways a teacher can provide feedback that encourages learning is to have students keep track of their own progress on topics. An easy way to do this is to provide students with a form like that shown in Figure 5.1 for each topic or selected topics addressed during a grading period. Each column in the line chart represents a different assessment for the topic *probability*. The first column represents the student's score on the first assessment, the second column represents the score on the second assessment, and so on. This technique provides students with a visual representation of their progress. It also provides a vehicle for students to establish their own learning goals and to define success in terms of their own learning as opposed to their standing relative to other students in the class. As discussed in Chapter 1, motivational psychologists such as Martin Covington (1992) believe that this simple change in perspective can help motivate students. In the parlance of motivational psychologists,

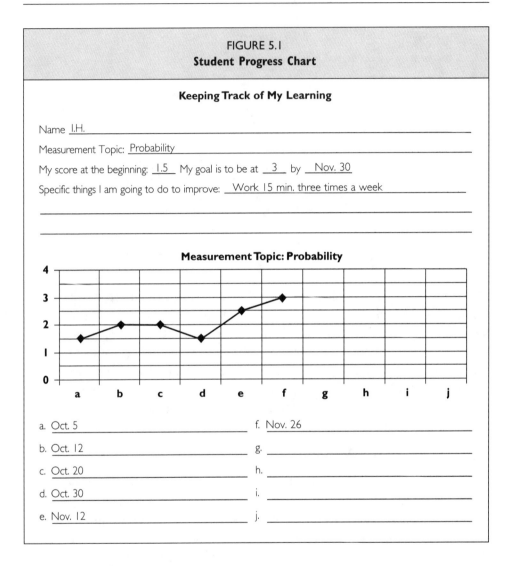

FIGURE 5.1
Student Progress Chart

Keeping Track of My Learning

Name I.H.

Measurement Topic: Probability

My score at the beginning: 1.5 My goal is to be at 3 by Nov. 30

Specific things I am going to do to improve: Work 15 min. three times a week

Measurement Topic: Probability

a. Oct. 5   f. Nov. 26

b. Oct. 12   g.

c. Oct. 20   h.

d. Oct. 30   i.

e. Nov. 12   j.

allowing students to see their "knowledge gain" throughout a grading period elicits "intrinsic" motivation.

Figure 5.2 illustrates how a teacher might track the progress of her four language arts classes. This chart is different in that it represents the percentage of students above a specific score point or "performance standard" for the measurement topic *effective paragraphs*. Chapter 3 addressed the concept of a performance standard. Briefly, it is the score on the scale (in this case the complete nine-point scale) that is the desired level of performance or understanding for all

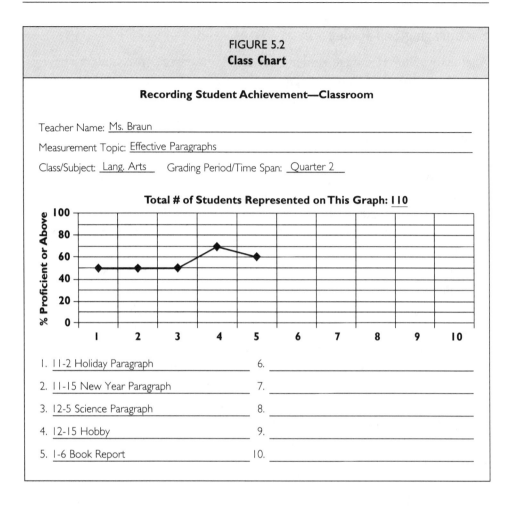

FIGURE 5.2
Class Chart

Recording Student Achievement—Classroom

Teacher Name: Ms. Braun

Measurement Topic: Effective Paragraphs

Class/Subject: Lang. Arts   Grading Period/Time Span: Quarter 2

Total # of Students Represented on This Graph: 110

% Proficient or Above

1. 11-2 Holiday Paragraph   6. _____
2. 11-15 New Year Paragraph   7. _____
3. 12-5 Science Paragraph   8. _____
4. 12-15 Hobby   9. _____
5. 1-6 Book Report   10. _____

students. In Figure 5.2, 50 percent of the students in Ms. Braun's class were at or above the performance standard on November 2, as they were for the next two assessments. However, by December 15, 70 percent of her students were at the performance standard or above.

This type of aggregated data can provide teachers and administrators with a snapshot of the progress of entire grade levels or an entire school. Individual teachers or teams of teachers can use such aggregated data to identify future instructional emphases. If the aggregated data indicate that an insufficient percentage of students in a particular grade level are at or above the designated performance standard, then the teachers at that grade level might mount a joint effort to enhance student progress for the measurement topic.

Encouraging Self-Reflection

Another way to encourage student learning is to ensure that students have an opportunity to reflect on their learning using information derived from classroom assessments. There are at least two ways to do this.

The first way to encourage self-reflection is to allow students to engage in self-assessment. Student self-assessment is mentioned quite frequently in the literature on classroom assessment (see Stiggins, Arter, Chappuis, & Chappuis, 2004), and a growing body of evidence supports its positive influence on student learning (Andrade & Boulay, 2003; Butler & Winne, 1995; Ross, Hogaboam-Gray, & Rolheiser, 2002). In the context of this book, self-assessment refers to students assigning their own scores for each assessment. For example, reconsider Figure 5.1, in which a student recorded the scores his teacher had given him for a series of classroom assessments. For each of these assessments, students could be invited to assign their own scores.

To facilitate self-assessment, the teacher can provide students with a simplified version of the scoring scale. Figure 5.3 presents student versions of the simplified five-point and complete nine-point scales.

One of the primary uses of student self-assessment is to provide a point of contrast with the teacher's assessment. Specifically, the teacher would compare the scores she gave to students on a particular assessment with the scores they gave themselves. Discrepancies provide an opportunity for teacher and students to interact. If a student scored himself higher than the teacher, the teacher would point out areas that need improvement before the student actually attained the score representing his perceived status. If the student scored himself lower than the teacher, the teacher would point out areas of strength the student might not be aware of.

A second way to stimulate self-reflection is to have students articulate their perceptions regarding their learning. K. Patricia Cross (1998) has developed a number of techniques to this end. For example, she offers the "minute paper" as a vehicle for self-reflection:

> Shortly before the end of a class period, the instructor asks students to write brief answers to these two questions: What is the most important thing that you learned in class today? and What is the main unanswered question you leave class with today? (p. 6)

A variation of the minute paper is the "muddiest point." Here students simply describe what they are most confused about in class. The teacher reads each

FIGURE 5.3
Student Versions of Scoring Scales

Simplified Scale		Complete Scale	
4.0	I know (can do) it well enough to make connections that weren't taught.	4.0	I know (can do) it well enough to make connections that weren't taught, and I'm right about those connections.
		3.5	I know (can do) it well enough to make connections that weren't taught, but I'm not always right about those connections.
3.0	I know (can do) everything that was taught without making mistakes.	3.0	I know (can do) everything that was taught (the easy parts and the harder parts) without making mistakes.
		2.5	I know (can do) all the easy parts and some (but not all) of the harder parts.
2.0	I know (can do) all the easy parts, but I don't know (can't do) the harder parts.	2.0	I know (can do) all the easy parts, but I don't know (can't do) the harder parts.
		1.5	I know (can do) some of the easier parts, but I make some mistakes.
1.0	With help, I know (can do) some of what was taught.	1.0	With help I know (can do) some of the harder parts and some of the easier parts.
		0.5	With help, I know (can do) some of the easier parts but not the harder parts.
0.0	I don't know (can't do) any of it	0.0	I don't know (can't do) any of it.

student's muddiest point and uses the information to plan further instruction and organize students into groups.

The student scales shown in Figure 5.3 can be used to help identify the muddiest point. To illustrate, consider the score of 2.0 on the simplified scale and the complete scale. Students who assign themselves this score are acknowledging that they are confused about some of the content. If students also were asked to describe what they find confusing, they would be identifying the muddiest points.

For Cross (1998), the most sophisticated form of reflection is the "diagnostic learning log," which involves students responding to four questions:

1. Briefly describe the assignment you just completed. What do you think was the purpose of this assignment?

2. Give an example of one or two of your most successful responses. Explain what you did that made them successful.

3. Provide an example of where you made an error or where your responses were less complete. Why were these items incorrect or less successful?

4. What can you do different when preparing next week's assignment? (p. 9)

Cross recommends that the teacher tabulate these responses, looking for patterns that will form the basis for planning future interactions with the whole class, groups of students, and individuals.

These examples illustrate the basic nature of self-reflection—namely, students commenting on their involvement and understanding of classroom tasks. Such behavior is what Deborah Butler and Philip Winne (1995) refer to as "self-regulated learning."

Focusing on Learning at the End of the Grading Period

The ultimate goal of assessing students on measurement topics is to estimate their learning at the end of the grading period. To illustrate, consider Figure 5.4, which shows one student's scores on five assessments over a nine-week period on the measurement topic *probability*. The student obtained a score of 1.0 on each of the first two assessments, 2.5 on the third, and so on. At the end of the grading period, the teacher will compute a final score that represents the student's performance on this topic. To do this, a common approach is to average the scores. In fact, one might say that K–12 education has a "bias" in favor of averaging. Many textbooks on classroom assessment explicitly or implicitly recommend averaging (see Airasian, 1994; Haladyna, 1999). As we shall see in the next chapter, in some situations computing an average makes sense. However, those situations generally do not apply to students' formative assessment scores over a period of time. Figure 5.5 helps to illustrate why this is so. As before, the bars represent the student's scores on each of the five assessments. The average—in this case 2.0—has been added, represented by the dashed line. To understand the implication of using the average of 2.0 as the final score for a student, recall the discussion in Chapter 3 about the concept of *true score*. Every score that a student receives on every assessment is made up of two parts—the true score and the error score. Ideally, the score a student receives on an assessment (referred to as the *observed score*) consists mostly of the student's true score. However, the error part of a student's score can dramatically alter the observed score. For example, a student might receive a score of 2.5 on an assessment but really deserve a

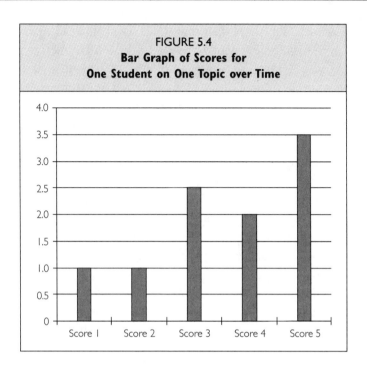

FIGURE 5.4
**Bar Graph of Scores for
One Student on One Topic over Time**

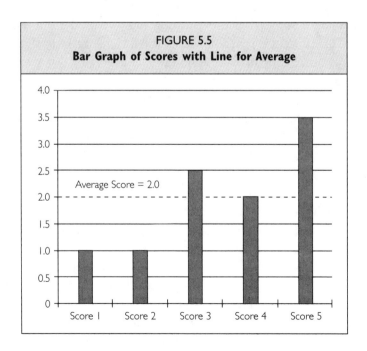

FIGURE 5.5
Bar Graph of Scores with Line for Average

3.0. The 0.5 error is due to the fact that the student misread or misunderstood some items on the assessment. Conversely, a student might receive a score of 2.5 but really deserve a 2.0 because she guessed correctly about some items.

The final score a student receives for a given measurement topic is best thought of as a final *estimate* of the student's true score for the topic. Returning to Figure 5.5, if we use the student's average score as an estimate of her true score at the end of a grading period, we would have to conclude that her true score is 2.0. This implies that the student has mastered the simple details and processes but has virtually no knowledge of the more complex ideas and processes. However, this interpretation makes little sense when we carefully examine all the scores over the grading period. In the first two assessments, the student's responses indicate that without help she could do little. However, from the third assessment on, the student never dropped below a score of 2.0, indicating that the simpler details and processes were not problematic. In fact, on the third assessment the student demonstrated partial knowledge of the complex information and processes, and on the fifth assessment the student demonstrated partial ability to go beyond what was addressed in class. Clearly in this instance the average of 2.0 does not represent the student's true score on the topic at the end of the grading period.

The main problem with averaging students' scores on formative assessments is that averaging assumes that no learning has occurred from assessment to assessment. This concept is inherent in classical test theory. Indeed, measurement theorists frequently define true score in terms of averaging test scores for a specific student. To illustrate, Frederic Lord (1959), architect of much of the initial thinking regarding classical test theory and item response theory, explains that the true score is "frequently defined as the average of the scores that the examinee would make on all possible parallel tests *if he did not change during the testing process* [emphasis added]" (p. 473). In this context, parallel tests can be thought of as those for which a student might have different observed scores but identical true scores. Consequently, when a teacher averages test scores for a given student, she is making the tacit assumption that the true score for the student is the same on each test. Another way of saying this is that use of the average assumes the differences in observed scores from assessment to assessment are simply a consequence of "random error," and the act of averaging will "cancel out" the random error from test to test (Magnusson, 1966, p. 64).

Unfortunately, the notion that a student's true score is the same from assessment to assessment contradicts what we know about learning and the formative assessments that are designed to track that learning. Learning theory and common sense tell us that a student might start a grading period with little or no knowledge regarding a topic but end the grading period with a great deal of knowledge. Learning theorists have described this phenomenon in detail. Specifically, one of the most ubiquitous findings in the research in cognitive psychology (for a discussion, see Anderson, 1995) is that learning resembles the curve shown in Figure 5.6. As depicted in the figure, the student in question begins with no understanding of the topic—with zero knowledge. Although this situation is probably never the case, or is at least extremely rare, it provides a useful perspective on the nature of learning. An interesting aspect of the learning curve is that the amount of learning from session to session is large at first—for example, it goes from zero to more than 20 percent after one learning session—but then it tapers off. In cognitive psychology, this trend in learning (introduced by Newell & Rosenbloom, 1981) is referred to as "the power law of learning" because the mathematical function describing the line in Figure 5.6 can be computed using a power function.

Technical Note 5.1 provides a more detailed discussion of the power law. Briefly, though, it has been used to describe learning in a wide variety of situations. Researcher John Anderson (1995) explains that "since its identification by Newell and Rosenbloom, the power law has attracted a great deal of attention in psychology, and researchers have tried to understand why learning should take the same form in all experiments" (p. 196). In terms of its application to formative assessment, the power law of learning suggests a great deal about the best estimate of a given student's true score at the end of a grading period. Obviously it supports the earlier discussion that the average score probably doesn't provide a good estimate of a student's score for a given measurement topic at the end of the grading period. In effect, using the average is tantamount to saying to a student, "I don't think you've learned over this grading period. The differences in your scores for this topic are due simply to measurement error."

The power law of learning also suggests another way of estimating the student's true score at the end of a grading period. Consider Figure 5.7, which depicts the score points for each assessment that one would estimate using the power law. That is, the first observed score for the student was 1.0; however, the power law estimates a true score of 0.85. The second observed score for the student was 1.0, but the power law estimates the true score to be 1.49, and so on. At the end of the grading period, the power law estimates the student's true score to be 3.07—much higher than the average score of 2.00. The power law makes these estimates by examining the pattern of the five observed scores over the grading period. (See Technical Note 5.1 for a discussion.) Given this pattern, it is

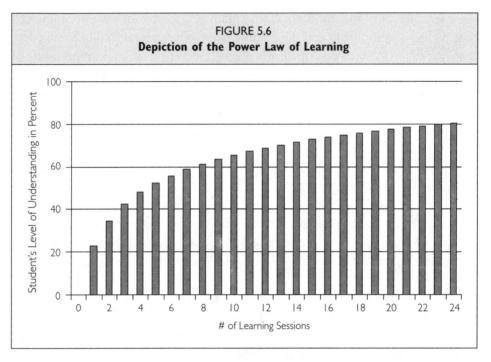

FIGURE 5.6
Depiction of the Power Law of Learning

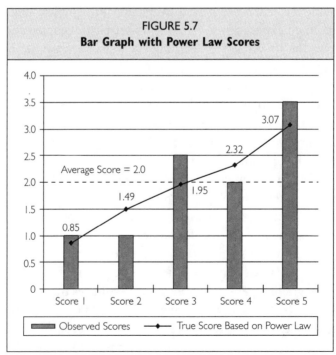

FIGURE 5.7
Bar Graph with Power Law Scores

FIGURE 5.8						
Comparisons of Observed Scores, Average Scores, and Estimated Power Law Scores						
Assessment	**1**	**2**	**3**	**4**	**5**	**Total Difference**
Observed Score	1.00	1.00	2.50	2.00	3.50	n/a
Average Score	2.00	2.00	2.00	2.00	2.00	n/a
Estimated Power Law Score	0.85	1.49	1.95	2.32	3.07	n/a
Difference Between Observed Score and Average Score	1.00	1.00	0.50	0.00	1.50	4.00
Difference Between Observed Score and Estimated Power Law Score	0.15	0.49	0.55	0.32	0.43	1.94

(mathematically) reasonable to assume that the second observed score of 1.0 had some error that artificially deflated the observed score, and the third observed score had some error that artificially inflated the observed score.

It is important to note that these estimates of the true score are just that—estimates. In fact, measurement theorists tell us that a student's true score on a given test is unobservable directly. We are always trying to estimate it (see Gulliksen, 1950; Lord & Novick, 1968; Magnusson, 1966). However, within a measurement topic, the final power law estimate of a student's true score is almost always superior to the true score estimate based on the average. To illustrate, consider Figure 5.8. The figure dramatizes the superiority of the power law as an estimate of a student's true scores over the average by contrasting the differences between the two true score estimates (average and power law) and the observed scores. For the first observed score of 1.00, the average estimates the true score to be 2.00, but the power law estimates the true score to be 0.85. The average is 1.00 units away from the observed score, and the power law estimate is 0.15 units away. For the second observed score of 1.00, the average estimates the true score to be 2.00 (the average will estimate the same true score for every observed score), but the power law estimates it to be 1.49. The average is 1.00 units away from the observed score, and the power law estimate is 0.49 units away. Looking at the last column in Figure 5.8, we see that the total differences between estimated and observed scores for the five assessments is 4.00 for the average and 1.94 for the power law. Taken as a set, the power law estimates are closer to the observed scores than are the estimates based on the average. The power law estimates "fit the observed data" better than the estimates based on the average. We will consider this concept of "best fit" again in Chapter 6.

The discussion thus far makes a strong case for using the power law to estimate each student's true score on each measurement topic at the end of a grading period. Obviously teachers should not be expected to do the necessary calculations on their own. In Chapter 6 we consider some technology solutions to this issue—computer software that does the calculations automatically. We might consider this the high-tech way of addressing the issue. However, teachers can also use a low-tech solution that does not require the use of specific computer software. I call this solution "the method of mounting evidence."

The Method of Mounting Evidence

The method of mounting evidence is fairly intuitive and straightforward. To follow it a teacher must use a grade book like that shown in Figure 5.9, which is different from the typical grade book. One obvious difference is that it has space for only about five students per page. (For ease of discussion, Figure 5.9 shows the scores for only one student.) Instead of one page accommodating all scores for a class of 30 students, this type of grade book would require six pages. A high school teacher working with five classes of 30 students each, or 150 students overall, would need a grade book with 30 pages—6 pages for each class. Although this

---

FIGURE 5.9
Grade Book for Method of Mounting Evidence

	Matter & Energy		Force & Motion	Reproduction & Heredity		Earth Processes		Adaptation	Behavior		Work Completion		Class Participation	
	1.5	2.5	2.0	1.0	2.5	2.0	3.0	3.0	3.0	3.5	4.0	3.5	2.5	3.5
	(2.0)		2.0	1.5		2.0		3.0	3.0	3.0	4.0	4.0	3.0	3.5
Aida	2.0		2.0	2.0		2.0		3.5	2.5	3.5	4.0	3.5	3.5	3.5
	2.0		(2.5)	(2.5)		(2.5)		3.5	3.0	3.5	3.5	4.0	3.0	4.0
	2.5		2.5	2.5		3.0		3.5	3.5		4.0		3.5	

Note: A circle indicates that the teacher gave the student an opportunity to raise his score from the previous assessment. A box indicates that the student is judged to have reached a specific score level from that point on.

is more pages than the traditional grade book, it is still not inordinate; and it is easy to create blank forms using standard word processing software. Additionally, it is important to keep in mind that a grade book like this should be considered an interim step only, used by teachers who simply wish to try out the system. Once a teacher becomes convinced that this system will be the permanent method of record keeping, then appropriate computer software can be purchased, as discussed in Chapter 6.

The columns in Figure 5.9 show the various measurement topics that the teacher is addressing over a given grading period. In this case the teacher has addressed five science topics: *matter and energy*, *force and motion*, *reproduction and heredity*, *earth processes*, and *adaptation*. The teacher has also kept track of the life skill topics *behavior*, *work completion*, and *class participation*. First we will consider the academic topics.

To illustrate how this grade book is used, consider Aida's scores for the topic *matter and energy*. In each cell of the grade book, the scores are listed in order of assignment, going from the top left to the bottom and the top right to the bottom. Thus, for *matter and energy* Aida has received six scores, in the following order: 1.5, 2.0, 2.0, 2.0, 2.5, and 2.5. Also note that the second score of 2.0 has a circle around it. This represents a situation in which the teacher gave Aida an opportunity to raise her score on a given assessment. This dynamic is at the heart of the method of mounting evidence. Aida received a score of 1.5 for the first assessment for this measurement topic. She demonstrated partial knowledge of the simpler aspects of the topic by correctly answering some Type I items but incorrectly answering other Type I items. However, after returning the assessment to Aida, the teacher talked with her and pointed out her errors on the Type I items, explaining why Aida's paper was scored a 1.5. The teacher also offered Aida the chance to demonstrate that her errors on the test for Type I items were not a true reflection of her understanding of the topic. In other words, the teacher offered Aida an opportunity to demonstrate that 1.5 was not an accurate reflection of her true score. The teacher might have allowed Aida to complete some exercises at the end of one of the textbook chapters that pertained to the topic, or she might have constructed some exercises that Aida could complete, or she might have asked Aida to devise a way to demonstrate her true knowledge.

Such an offer is made to students when their scores on a particular assessment for a particular topic are not consistent with their behavior in class. For example, perhaps in class discussions about matter and energy, Aida has exhibited an understanding of the basic details and processes, indicating that she deserves a score of 2.0. The results on the first assessment, then, don't seem consistent with the informal information the teacher has gained about Aida in class. The teacher uses this earlier knowledge of Aida to guide her evaluation regarding this particular topic. Based on this prior knowledge, the teacher has decided that she needs to gather more evidence about Aida's level of understanding and skill on this particular topic. Notice that the teacher doesn't simply change the score on the assessment. Rather, she gives Aida an opportunity to provide more information about this particular measurement topic. If the new information provided by Aida corroborates the teacher's perception that Aida is at level 2.0 for the topic, the teacher changes the score in the grade book and circles it to indicate that it represents a judgment based on additional information.

Another convention to note in Figure 5.9 is that some scores—such as Aida's fourth score of 2.0—are enclosed in a box. When a teacher uses this convention it means that she has seen enough evidence to conclude that a student has reached a certain point on the scale. By the time the teacher entered the fourth score for Aida, she was convinced that Aida had attained a score of 2.0. From that assessment on, the teacher examined Aida's responses for evidence that she has *exceeded* this score. That is, from that point on, the teacher examined Aida's assessments for evidence that she deserved a score greater than a 2.0. This does not mean that Aida is allowed to miss Type I items. Indeed, any assessment on which Aida does not correctly answer Type I items would be returned to her with the directions that she must correct her errors in a way that demonstrates the accuracy of her assigned score of 2.0. However, the teacher would consider these errors to be lapses in effort or reasoning or both, as opposed to an indication that Aida's true score is less than 2.0.

The underlying dynamic of the method of mounting evidence, then, is that once a student has provided enough evidence for the teacher to conclude that a certain score level has been reached, that score is considered the student's true score for the topic at that point in time. Using this as a foundation, the teacher seeks evidence for the next score level up. Once enough evidence has been gathered, the teacher concludes that this next score level represents the true score, and so on until the end of the grading period. Mounting evidence, then, provides the basis for a decision that a student has reached a certain level of understanding or skill.

This approach has a strong underlying logic and can be supported from various research and theoretical perspectives. First, recall from Figure 1.2 in Chapter 1 that a gain of 20 percentile points is associated with the practice of asking students to repeat an activity until they demonstrate they can do it correctly. The method of mounting evidence certainly has aspects of this "mastery-oriented" approach. Indeed, some of the early work of Benjamin Bloom (1968, 1976, 1984) and Tom Guskey (1980, 1985, 1987, 1996a) was based on a similar approach. The method of mounting evidence can also be supported from the perspective of a type of statistical inference referred to as "Bayesian inference." For a more thorough discussion of Bayesian inference, see Technical Note 5.2. Briefly, though, Bayesian inference takes the perspective that the best estimate of a student's true score at any point in time must take into consideration what we know about the student from past experiences. Each assessment is not thought of as an isolated piece of information; rather, each assessment is evaluated from the perspective of what is already known about the student relative to a specific measurement topic. In a sense, Bayesian inference asks the question, "Given what is known about the student regarding this measurement topic, what is the best estimate of her true score on this assessment?" It is a generative form of evaluation that seeks more information when a teacher is uncertain about a specific score on a specific assessment.

The Life Skill Topics

Life skill topics might also be approached from the method of mounting evidence, but with a slight variation on the theme. Consider Aida's life skill scores in Figure 5.9. These scores are not tied to specific assessments. As mentioned in Chapter 4, once a week the teacher has scored students on these three topics, perhaps using the last few minutes of class each Friday. The teacher has recorded nine scores for *behavior*, one for each week of the grading period. Again, the scores are entered from the top left to the bottom, and then from the top right to the bottom. Thus, Aida's scores in the order in which they were assigned are 3.0, 3.0, 2.5, 3.0, 3.5, 3.5, 3.0, 3.5, and 3.5. Notice that a number of these scores have been enclosed in a box. Again, the box signifies that the teacher judges it to be the student's true score at a particular moment in time. Therefore, Aida's second score of 3.0, which is enclosed in a box, indicates that at that point in time the teacher concluded it to be Aida's true score for *behavior*. Notice that the next score is a 2.5—a half point lower than the teacher's estimate the previous week (assuming life skill scores are recorded every week on Friday). Given the drop in performance, the teacher met with Aida and told her that she must bring her score back up to a 3.0 by the next week. In this case, Aida did just that. The teacher then enclosed that next score in a box to reaffirm that 3.0 was, in fact, Aida's true score.

Summary and Conclusions

Effective formative assessment should encourage students to improve. Three techniques can help accomplish this goal. The first involves students tracking their progress on specific measurement topics using graphs. The second engages students in different forms of self-reflection regarding their progress on measurement topics. The third addresses estimating students' true scores at the end of a grading period. In particular, the practice of averaging scores on formative assessments is a questionable way to produce a valid estimate of final achievement status. Two alternatives are preferable. One uses the power law to estimate students' final status. The second uses mounting evidence to estimate students' final status.

6

Final Scores and Grades

Arguably the most well entrenched tradition in U.S. education is the overall grade. More than a decade ago, Lynn Olson (1995) observed that grades are "one of the most sacred traditions in American education. . . . The truth is that grades have acquired an almost cult-like importance in American schools. They are the primary shorthand tool for communicating to parents how children are faring" (p. 24). More recently, grading expert Susan Brookhart (2004) echoed the same sentiment when she noted that "in a perfect world there would be no need for the kind of grades we use in school today. . . . [But] grades are not going to disappear from schools anytime soon" (p. 4). In this chapter we consider the most valid and useful ways to construct an overall grade. We begin with a discussion of the type of computer software necessary for an effective system of formative assessments.

In Chapter 5, I referred to the "high-tech" solution to recording scores on measurement topics. Obviously, one requirement for a classroom assessment system like the one described in this book is computer software that allows for the efficient entry and processing of student scores on formative assessments for a variety of measurement topics. Many software packages are available that allow teachers to enter student scores in traditional categories such as quizzes, homework, midterms, and the like. However, these software packages typically do not allow for tracking and processing of scores on specific measurement topics, particularly for formative assessments. This chapter describes the following three characteristics of a software system that would accommodate the use of formative assessments as described in the book:

• The software should allow teachers to establish multiple measurement topics of their own design and easy entry of scores for those topics.

• The software should provide for the most accurate representation of a student's score on each measurement topic at the end of the grading period.

• The software should provide graphs and tables of students' scores.

The Pinnacle Plus system developed by Excelsior Software is a software system that exemplifies these characteristics.* If other software programs perform the functions described in this chapter and alluded to in previous chapters, I am not aware of them.

Multiple Measurement Topics and Easy Entry of Scores

The most obvious requirement for a software system suited to formative assessments is that it allows teachers to establish multiple measurement topics and enter scores for specific students for each topic. As noted, some programs have predetermined categories such as homework, quizzes, midterms, and so on. Although these categories might be relabeled to represent measurement topics as described in this book, it is best if the software is designed specifically for this function.

Using the Pinnacle Plus system, one of the first things teachers do is identify the academic and life skill measurement topics they will keep track of throughout a grading period. The system also allows teachers to refer to these topics using their own terminology or that used by the school. For example, teachers might refer to their topics as *power standards*, *critical learning standards*, *essential skills*, *learner outcomes*, and so on.

The system also allows teachers to collapse measurement topics into larger categories. For example, a language arts teacher might keep track of six measurement topics. In addition to keeping track of formative assessment scores on each of the six topics, the teacher might wish to collapse the scores on three of the topics into a category referred to as Reading. The other three topics might be collapsed into a category referred to as Writing.

After defining measurement topics and collapsing them into categories, the teacher can easily enter scores on assessments into the grade book. To illustrate, assume that a 5th grade mathematics teacher is keeping track of six mathematics measurement topics (*probability*, *data analysis and distributions*, *central tendency and dispersion*, *measurement*, *problem solving*, and *patterns and functions*) and three life skill topics (*work completion*, *participation*, and *behavior*), for a total of nine

---

*Editor's note: Readers should be aware that ASCD endorses Pinnacle Plus and, at the time of this writing, believes it to be the only software currently available that can be used to implement the author's recommended approach to data analysis. Nevertheless, the technical notes for this chapter are provided for districts who wish to program their own data analysis system.

	FIGURE 6.1		
	Pinnacle Plus View for Entering Scores on Assessments		
Student Name	**Test #1 Probability**	**Test #2 Probability**	**Test #2 Patterns & Functions**
Aida	3.0	3.5	3.0
Ashley	2.0	2.5	2.5
Carmen	2.5	3.0	3.0
Cecilia	3.0	3.5	3.0
Christina	1.5	2.5	2.0
Jana	1.0	1.5	2.5
Julia	3.0	3.0	3.0
Mark	2.5	3.0	3.5
Todd	0.5	1.0	2.5
Whitney	3.0	2.5	3.5

topics. The teacher has designed and scored an assessment that addresses two topics: (1) *probability* and (2) *patterns and functions*. Each student's paper has two scale scores—one for each topic. The teacher now enters each student's set of scores into the system. The teacher would have first defined the fact that this particular assessment addressed two measurement topics. When the teacher is ready to enter students' scores for the test, a screen like that shown in Figure 6.1 would appear. In the figure, each row represents a student, and each column represents a measurement topic on a given assessment. The assessment the teacher has just scored (covering two topics) is represented by the third and fourth columns. The second column contains scores on a previous assessment (Test #1), which addressed a single topic, *probability*. The teacher can label an assessment in any fashion she wishes and link any measurement topic to any assessment.

The whole-class view shown in Figure 6.1 allows the teacher to enter scores for all students at one time. (The view in the Pinnacle Plus system contains enough rows to enter scores for 50 students in a single class.) A drop-down menu with all full-point and half-point scores for the complete nine-point scale allows the teacher to simply select the appropriate scale score for each student on each topic, as opposed to typing the numerals and decimal points. Also, the view depicted in Figure 6.1 is always available so that the teacher can examine any student's scores on all assessments within a grading period at any time.

Accurate Representations of Scores at the End of the Grading Period

In Chapter 5 we saw that the average score for a given measurement topic is not necessarily the best representation of a student's true score at the end of a grading period. We also saw that an estimated true score based on what is called the "power law of learning" is typically a better estimate. Effective software should provide teachers with an estimate of the student's final true score based on the power law, a score that is based on the average, and a way of determining which estimate best fits the data.

To illustrate, consider the set of scores in Figure 6.2. As described in Chapter 5, the average estimates the true score to be the same on each assessment occasion. In Figure 6.2, the average estimates the student's true score to be 2.10 for the first assessment, the second assessment, and so on. The power law provides a far different estimate. It estimates the true score to be 0.49 for the first assessment, 1.64 for the second assessment, and culminates in a final estimate of 3.65 for the fifth assessment. As we saw in Chapter 5, the true score estimates based on the average and the power law can be contrasted in terms of how well they "fit" the data. This is done by computing the difference between each predicted true score estimate and the observed score and then summing these differences. These quantities are shown in the bottom section of Figure 6.2. As before, the estimates based on the power law are closer to the observed scores. Specifically, the total distance of the average from the observed scores is 4.60, and the total distance of the power law scores from the observed scores is 0.62. Thus, the power law scores "fit" the observed data better. A software program should compute these quantities for each measurement topic and use these quantities to identify the better of the two estimates—the one based on the power law or the one based on the average. The Pinnacle Plus system performs these calculations and uses the best-fitting estimate of the true score unless the teacher overrides this mathematical selection.

A reasonable question one might ask is, when would the average be a better estimate of a student's true score than the power law estimate? When learning takes place, won't the average always underestimate a student's true score for a given measurement topic? The answer is yes, but in some instances the average is more appropriate. To illustrate, consider the following pattern of scores: 2.0, 3.0, 1.5, 2.5, and 2.0. From a learning perspective, this pattern makes little sense. The student started with a score of 2.0, which indicates competence in the simpler details and processes but major errors and omissions in the more complex ideas and processes. The second score, 3.0, indicates competence in the simpler

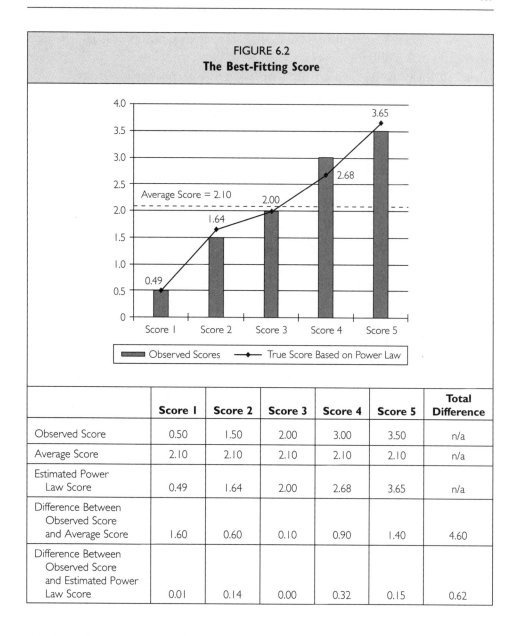

FIGURE 6.2
The Best-Fitting Score

	Score 1	**Score 2**	**Score 3**	**Score 4**	**Score 5**	**Total Difference**
Observed Score	0.50	1.50	2.00	3.00	3.50	n/a
Average Score	2.10	2.10	2.10	2.10	2.10	n/a
Estimated Power Law Score	0.49	1.64	2.00	2.68	3.65	n/a
Difference Between Observed Score and Average Score	1.60	0.60	0.10	0.90	1.40	4.60
Difference Between Observed Score and Estimated Power Law Score	0.01	0.14	0.00	0.32	0.15	0.62

details and processes as well as the more complex ideas and processes. Together these two scores give the impression that the student is learning the knowledge associated with the topic very quickly. The trend in learning is steep. However, the third score in the sequence breaks this pattern. The 1.5 signifies that the student demonstrates partial knowledge of the simpler ideals and processes and major misconceptions regarding the more complex ideas and processes. The next two scores of 2.5 and 2.0 continue this uneven pattern. How can such a pattern occur? At least two reasons explain why uneven patterns may occur.

The first reason is measurement error. Recall from the discussion in Chapters 4 and 5 that measurement error occurs for many reasons, such as a student misinterpreting items on the test or the items themselves being ambiguous. Another source of measurement error is the teacher misreading or misinterpreting the student's responses. Still another source of measurement error is recording. The teacher intends to write a score of 3.0 on a student's paper but writes a 2.0 instead. Finally, measurement error might be caused by a student's lack of effort. If a student tries to do well on one assessment but not on another, the score on the second assessment will probably not reflect the student's true score for the topic being assessed.

A second reason why scores for a given measurement topic might exhibit an uneven pattern has to do with the measurement topic itself. Recall from Chapter 2 that a measurement topic should contain elements that are either unidimensional or so closely related that competence in one element is strongly associated with competence in another element. We referred to this characteristic as *covariance*. As competence in one area increases, so does competence in another area. When a district or a school designs measurement topics, its goal should be to ensure that all elements within a topic exhibit this relationship—strong covariance. Sometimes this goal is not met, and when this occurs, the precision of measurement for the topic in question suffers. To illustrate, consider the measurement topic *reading for the main idea*, introduced in Chapter 2. Assume that at the 6th grade a district identified the following as an indication of a score of 3.0:

> While reading grade-appropriate material, the student identifies and describes
>
> 1. complex causal relationships that are explicit and implied,
> 2. basic arguments that are explicit and implied,
> 3. plots with single story lines that are explicit and implied,
> 4. terminology that is based on mythology, and
> 5. technical terminology.
>
> The student exhibits no major errors or omissions.

Elements 1, 2, and 3 seem to be related—they address the ability to recognize and describe organizational patterns. If you can do one, there is a good chance you can do the other. However, elements 4 and 5 don't seem to fit well. They deal with understanding different types of terms. Consequently, a student might perform well on elements 4 or 5 but not on elements 1, 2, or 3. In the terminology of Chapter 2, this measurement topic is *multidimensional,* and the dimensions do not *covary.* This might cause an uneven pattern of scores, like the pattern mentioned earlier: 2.0, 3.0, 1.5, 2.5, and 2.0. The first assessment is on element 1. The next assessment is on element 2, which is related to element 1. In fact, the student is getting better quite quickly at her ability to identify organizational patterns. However, the third assessment is on element 4, which is not related to element 1 or 2. The student's score on this assessment is very low, not because the student has lost proficiency at recognizing organizational patterns, but because a new dimension unrelated to the first two has been introduced.

When measurement error or the multidimensional nature of a topic is the cause of uneven score patterns, the best representation of the overall pattern of the data is the average as opposed to the power law score. Thus, grading software needs to provide an average score and a power law score for each measurement topic, and it should identify the one that best fits the data.

Graphs and Tables of Students' Scores

In Chapter 5 we explored the idea of students keeping track of their progress on measurement topics by generating their own graphs and the potential benefits of this activity. In addition to these student-generated graphs, grading software should produce computer-generated graphs quickly and efficiently for any measurement topic at any time. To illustrate, consider Figure 6.3, which depicts a graph generated by the Pinnacle Plus system for a specific student on a specific measurement topic. Like Figure 6.2, Figure 6.3 provides a bar graph representing each observed score for a measurement topic, the scores predicted using the power law, and a line representing the average. Graphs like this one can be produced and printed for each measurement topic for each student. A teacher could use the graph to enhance the conversation during a student-teacher conference, perhaps printing out a hard copy for the student to keep and also sending a copy to the student's parents.

Figure 6.4 shows another type of report a software system should generate. The report is for an individual student, and it includes the academic measurement topics only. Another view could be provided for the life skill topics, and still another including both.

This report doesn't show bar graphs for each measurement topic, nor does it have a line representing the power law scores. However, it does provide a comprehensive picture of all measurement topics and the scores to date. In a sense, this view is a panorama of a particular student's scores on all assessments on all

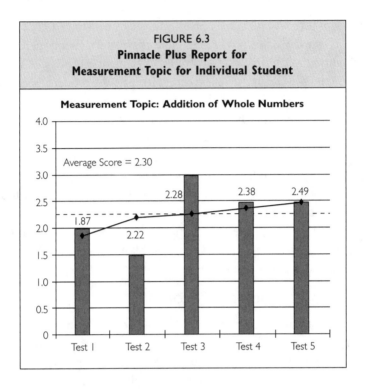

FIGURE 6.3
Pinnacle Plus Report for
Measurement Topic for Individual Student

Measurement Topic: Addition of Whole Numbers

measurement topics. The assessment key at the top of the report shows when each assessment was given. Note that the teacher has referred to some assessments as "assignments" and others as "tests." As described in Chapter 5, an assessment can take many forms, including traditional paper-and-pencil tests and assignments that might begin in class but be completed at home. The report in Figure 6.4 also provides a final score for each topic. As discussed previously, this score would be either the final power law score or the average—whichever best fits the data.

Reports like those depicted in Figures 6.3 and 6.4 are tools to stimulate dialogue among teachers, students, and parents. When used for such purposes, they are a valuable part of the assessment process.

Common Questions and Issues

Over the years that the system presented in this book has been developed, a number of issues have surfaced consistently, and four questions typically emerge. The questions deal with weighting of assessments, the number of assessments that should be given, how to approach quizzes, and the overall accuracy of the system.

		FIGURE 6.4				
		Measurement Topic View				

Student: Jana

Assessment Key

1. Assignment Sept. 10	6. Assignment Sept. 24	11. Assignment Oct. 13
2. Test Sept. 13	7. Assignment Sept. 29	12. Test Oct. 15
3. Assignment Sept. 17	8. Test Oct. 2	13. Assignment Oct. 17
4. Test Sept. 20	9. Test Oct. 5	14. Final #1 Oct. 26
5. Test Sept. 22	10. Assignment Oct. 10	15. Final #2 Nov. 1

	Probability	Data Analysis & Distributions	Central Tendency & Dispersion	Measurement	Problem Solving	Patterns & Functions
1	.5	1.0				
2	1.5	.5				
3			2.0	1.0		
4	2.0	2.5				
5			1.5	1.0		
6					1.0	.5
7			3.0	2.0		
8	3.0	1.5				
9						1.5
10			2.5	2.0		
11					1.5	
12					2.0	
13						2.0
14	3.5	2.0			2.5	2.5
15			2.5	3.0	3.0	3.5
Final Score	3.65	1.71	2.49	2.41	2.80	3.65

What About Weighting?

When presented with this system, some teachers ask why one assessment is not weighted more than another assessment. After all, shouldn't the final examination count more than a quiz? In this system, weighting makes little sense, and, in fact, there is no way mathematically to use the power law if assessments are weighted. This is not to say that all assessments are the same. Indeed, the reason teachers typically weight one assessment more than another is easily addressed within this system.

Most assessments that receive more weight than others address multiple topics. For example, a quiz will receive a low weight because it addresses one topic only. A 5th grade mathematics teacher might give four quizzes, each addressing the topic *computation*. Each quiz is assigned 10 points only. However, the final examination has items that address all five topics covered in the quarter. Within a traditional record-keeping system, the teacher would probably assign the final examination more points than a quiz.

Within the system presented in this book, the final examination would be weighted automatically because it would include five scores—one for each topic that was addressed. Each score would be entered under its appropriate topic. In effect, then, the final has received greater weight than a quiz because it carries information about five topics, whereas a quiz carries information about one topic. To illustrate, consider the entries in Figure 6.4 for Final #1 on October 26 and Final #2 on November 1. This teacher administered two finals—one covering four topics on October 26 and the other covering four topics on November 1. In effect, these two assessments received twice the weight of any other assessment.

How Many Assessments Should Be Administered?

Another frequently asked question deals with the number of assessments that are needed to provide a good estimate of a student's true score at the end of the grading period. Technical Note 6.1 provides a more detailed discussion of this issue, including how assessment should be spaced throughout a grading period. Briefly, though, from a mathematical perspective, at least three scores are required to estimate the power law score. However, from a measurement perspective, I usually recommend at least four assessments per topic per grading period, and ideally five. As we saw in Chapter 4, this does not mean that a teacher must administer five formal pencil-and-paper assessments for each topic. Rather, a teacher might use scores from informal assessments such as probing discussions or even selected homework assignments to obtain multiple scores on each student for each measurement topic.

A general rule to follow is this: The less certain you are about a student's true score on a given topic, the more assessment information you should collect. Consequently, for a certain student, a teacher might feel confident that the student's score on a given topic is 4.0 after only three assessments. For another student, the teacher might be quite unsure about the student's true score after the same three assessments. The uncertainty might be due to a highly uneven pattern of responses. In that case, the teacher would seek out more information by asking the student to complete more exercises or engaging the student in probing discussions. The teacher would treat this information as added assessments and enter it into the grade book.

Along with the number of scores that should be obtained, a related issue is the spacing of those scores. To most accurately compute the power law scores shown in Figures 6.3 and 6.4, one must take into account when specific scores were obtained. To illustrate, assume that a teacher obtains a score for a particular measurement topic for each student on the first day of a new grading period. She administers additional assessments after one week, three weeks, seven weeks, and nine weeks. The teacher has obtained five scores for the measurement topic, but they represent different points in the learning process. Mathematically, these differences can be accounted for when computing the power law estimates of the true scores. Again, Technical Note 6.1 explains how this is done. Relative to the discussion here, the implication is that the computer software should make this adjustment. In fact, if power law scores are computed without the adjustment for time differences between assessments, the scores will be biased estimates of students' true scores.

Another issue related to the number of assessments that should be provided is what to do about students who do not take an assessment or fail to turn in an assignment that is to be used as an assessment. One absolute rule within the system presented in this book is that *the student should not be assigned a score of zero for not taking a test, not turning in an assignment, or turning it in late.* The negative consequences of including a score of zero for failure to take a test or failure to hand in an assignment have been discussed thoroughly by Thomas Guskey and Jane Bailey (2001) and Douglas Reeves (2004). Briefly, though, including in a set of scores a zero that is not a legitimate estimate of a student's true score renders both the power law estimate and the average meaningless. This is not to say that a teacher should ignore a student's unwillingness to turn in assignments. Indeed, if the district or school has identified *work completion* as one of the life skill topics, the extent to which students fulfill their responsibility regarding assignments can be recorded on a regular basis.

To illustrate, consider the scale in Figure 6.5, which was introduced in slightly different form in Chapter 4. If each assignment is scored using the scale in Figure 6.5, the teacher will have a detailed history of each student's behavior relative to the life skill topic *work completion*. At the end of the grading period, the teacher can compute a final score for this life skill. For behaviorally oriented topics such as this, I commonly recommend using the average as the estimate of

---

FIGURE 6.5
Scoring Scale for the Life Skill Topic *Work Completion*

4.0	In addition to level 3.0 performance, the student goes beyond the required conventions.
3.0	The student hands in work on time and meets all required conventions.
2.0	With some noteworthy exceptions, the student hands in work on time and meets required conventions.
1.0	With help or prodding, the student hands in work on time and meets required conventions.
0.0	Even with help or prodding, the student does not hand in work on time or meet required conventions.

---

a student's true score rather than the score based on the power law, because such things as handing in assignments on time using the proper conventions might be more a matter of student responsibility than skill. Over a grading period, students might be more or less responsible at different times. In other words, their previous behavior relative to assignments might not indicate what they will do regarding the next assignment. In such cases, the average will be a better final score for students' behavior throughout the grading period than the power law score. Nevertheless, the power score should be used if the teacher believes it is the better representation of a student's behavior.

As mentioned, I recommend at least four assessments and ideally five for each measurement topic. If a student has been absent for a number of assessments, I recommend that the burden of providing compensatory assessment information be shifted to the student. That is, the teacher might tell the student that she needs more information about the student's understanding and skill regarding a specific topic before making a decision about a final score. The teacher might direct the student to some additional exercises in the textbook or ask the student to suggest options for how this additional assessment information will be provided.

What About Quizzes?

One issue that frequently arises when a system like the one described in this book is implemented is how to address quizzes that do not allow students to demonstrate all levels of the complete scoring scale. Recall that to obtain a score of 2.0 a student must demonstrate full knowledge of the simpler details and processes. To obtain a score of 2.5 a student must demonstrate full knowledge of the simpler details and processes and partial knowledge of the more complex ideas and processes. Consequently, if a quiz addresses the simpler details and processes only (i.e., the quiz contains only Type I items), the highest score a student can receive using the complete scale is 2.0. There are at least three ways to address this issue.

The most straightforward approach is to include a few Type II and Type III items on every quiz. This convention would allow students to demonstrate knowledge at level 2.5 and above on every quiz even though the focus of each quiz would be the simpler details and processes. The teacher would explain to students that the Type II and III items should be considered as "extra," to be completed only after the items addressing the basic details and processes have been completed. In short, adding some Type II and Type III items to every quiz allows students to demonstrate the full range of understanding and skill on every assessment, alleviating the problem of quizzes having a "ceiling" score of 2.0.

If a teacher does not wish to include some Type II and Type III items on every quiz, then quizzes with the 2.0 ceiling can be administered only at the beginning of a grading period. For example, a teacher might plan to have three quizzes at the beginning of the grading period on a specific measurement topic, followed by three assessments at the end of the grading period that have Type II and III items, allowing for score values up to 4.0. The highest score students could receive on the first three assessments (quizzes) is 2.0, but the highest score that students could receive on the last three assessments is 4.0. Given that the power law does not excessively penalize students for their lack of understanding or skill at the beginning of a learning situation, the final estimated true score for a student will not be inordinately affected by the scores on the quizzes that have a ceiling.

To illustrate, assume that a student received scores of 2.0 on the three quizzes and scores of 4.0 on the three assessments at the end of the grading period. Also assume that those scores were evenly spaced throughout the grading period. The power law would estimate the student's true score at the end of the grading period to be 3.57. Although it is true that this is an underestimate of the true score, the teacher, realizing that the student received a perfect score on all assessments, would simply change the final estimated score to a 4.0.

This example underscores the fact that calculations like the power law and the average are tools that are based on certain assumptions. Realizing that certain assumptions have not been met, a teacher need only adjust final true score estimates up or down to account for the fact that the mathematical models on which the average and power law scores are based do not fit the data perfectly.

The third (and least favorable) way to address quizzes is to place all scores on quizzes in a separate category. That is, a separate measurement topic would be created for quizzes. I consider this option the least favorable because a category is created that is not based on covarying elements. Rather, a "quizzes" category is

---

FIGURE 6.6
Scoring Scale for Quizzes

4.0   Student answers all items on the quiz correctly.

3.0   Student exhibits minor errors and/or misses very few items.

2.0   Student exhibits major errors and/or misses many items.

1.0   With help, student answers some items correctly.

0.0   Even with help, student answers no items correctly.

---

simply an artifact of adherence to a rather antiquated (I believe) system of assessment. These concerns notwithstanding, in this situation I recommend that teachers use the scale in Figure 6.6, or an adaptation of it, to score all quizzes. The scale in Figure 6.6 is an obvious adaptation of the simplified scale introduced in Chapter 3. It allows for quizzes to be scored on a scale with a maximum value of 4.0. Score values of 0.0 and 1.0 are basically the same as before. A score of 4.0 indicates that the student has answered all items correctly. A score of 3.0 indicates minor errors, and a score of 2.0 indicates major errors. As before, the scale requires teachers to make judgments about students' levels of understanding and skill. The teacher does not simply add up the points on a quiz. As we saw in previous chapters, such judgments are the heart of *evaluation*, which is critical to a sound system of formative assessments.

How Accurate Is This System?

A very reasonable question to ask is, how accurate is this system? The issue of accuracy was partially addressed in Chapter 3 in the discussion of reliability. Here we consider this issue in more depth. In Chapter 3 we noted that studies have shown that the reliability of a score obtained by a single teacher using the scale presented in this book is .719, whereas the reliability of a score obtained using the point system is .294. Additionally, when two teachers independently score an assessment using the scale, the combined score has a reliability of .822. If four teachers independently score each assessment, the reliability of the combined score is .901.

This finding implies that a school or district could use teacher-designed assessments to obtain scores for students that rival standardized and state tests in their accuracy. For example, a district or school might construct and administer one assessment per semester that covers all the topics addressed in a given subject area. If two teachers independently scored each assessment, expected reliabilities for the scores would be high. Teachers would use the scores on these assessments as added information for estimating students' final status on measurement topics. However, the district or school would also use these scores to obtain aggregated data across different grade levels, student groups, and so on. This aggregated data could be used to set instructional goals for the entire district, for the entire school, or for specific classes.

Another aspect of reliability that should be considered is the reliability of the final estimate of a student's true score on a specific topic. This issue has been the subject of much discussion in the literature on measurement (see Collins & Sayer, 2001). Technical Note 6.2 addresses this issue is some detail. Briefly, the reliability of an estimate of a student's true score using the power law can be computed by examining how far away each estimate is from the observed scores within a grading period. We addressed this issue earlier when we considered how to determine whether the average or the power law provides the best estimate of the final true score. Here the differences between observed and estimated scores serve a different purpose. In simple terms, the closer the estimated scores for each student are to the observed scores, the higher the reliability of the final true score estimate. In a study I conducted (Marzano, 2006), the reliability of estimates of final true scores for a group of 25 students was found to be .67. Again, this is relatively high when compared with other forms of assessment. Also, examining the reliability of final true score estimates provides a second way to consider the overall accuracy of judgments about students. That is, typically only the reliability of individual assessments is considered. Little discussion is ever focused on the reliability of aggregated data from a set of scores for a given student. Using formative assessment as described in this book allows for the analysis of reliability from two perspectives—individual assessments and final true score estimates.

The Final Grade

Once final scores have been estimated for each measurement topic, the teacher can compute an overall grade. Chapter 7 provides alternatives to the overall grade. In fact, a case will be made that an overall grade is relatively meaningless from a measurement perspective. However, overall grades will probably be the norm in most schools for some time to come. Recall the quotation from Lynn Olson (1995) at the beginning of this chapter, stating that "grades have acquired an almost cult-like importance in American schools" (p. 24). Consequently, if a district or school wishes to assign overall grades, the software system it uses should allow for this to be done easily and efficiently.

The most straightforward approach to assigning an overall grade is to weight the final score for each measurement topic, as exemplified in Figure 6.7. The figure shows that the teacher has kept track of nine topics throughout the grading period—six mathematics topics and three life skill topics. The teacher has assigned a weight of 1 to all topics except *probability, central tendency and dispersion,* and *problem solving.* In effect, these three topics receive twice as much weight as all others.

From this weighting scheme, the teacher can compute an overall weighted score, as shown in Figure 6.8. As the figure shows, the final topic scores are reported in half-point increments coinciding with the complete scale. I recommend this convention instead of reporting the exact value computed using the power law or the average. To illustrate, assume that the power law computes a final topic score of 2.65, and it is determined that this value fits the data better than the average. Although a value of 2.65 might seem more precise than the half-point value of 2.5 or 3.0, it is important to remember that the overall goal is to estimate a student's true score as accurately and rigorously as possible. Although allowing for scores of 2.65 or 2.66 or 2.67 might seem more accurate because more score values are possible (actually, an infinite number of values is possible), a strong case can be made that using half-point scores is more precise. This is because a score of 2.5 (or 1.0 or 1.5 and so on) can be explained in terms of levels of understanding and skill—the student knows the basics and has partial knowledge of the more complex ideas for a specific topic. However, it is difficult

FIGURE 6.7
Weights Assigned to Topics

Measurement Topic	Weight
Probability	2
Data Analysis & Distributions	1
Central Tendency & Dispersion	2
Measurement	1
Problem Solving	2
Patterns & Functions	1
Work Completion	1
Participation	1
Behavior	1

FIGURE 6.8 The Weighted Average			
Measurement Topic	**Final Topic Score**	**Weight**	**Quality Points**
Probability	3.5	2	7.0
Data Analysis & Distributions	2.5	1	2.5
Central Tendency & Dispersion	2.5	2	5.0
Measurement	1.5	1	1.5
Problem Solving	3.0	2	6.0
Patterns & Functions	2.0	1	2.0
Work Completion	2.5	1	2.5
Participation	2.5	1	2.5
Behavior	3.5	1	3.5
Totals	n/a	12	32.5

to explain what a score of 2.65 means in terms of understanding and skill. (Does a score of 2.65 mean that a student has 0.05 more knowledge than a student with a score of 2.60?) Consequently, I recommend that teachers translate the final topic score computed by the power law or average into the half-point scale that is the most probable representation of a student's true score. In many cases this amounts to rounding to the closest half-point score. For example, a final topic score of 2.65 computed by the power law would be rounded to a score of 2.5. Rounding should not be done thoughtlessly, however. That is, a score of 2.74 should not automatically be rounded to a 2.5, and a score of 2.76 should not automatically be rounded to a 3.0. The decision as to the final half-point score on a topic should be based on the teacher's best judgment, using all available information.

One other important qualification applies to Figure 6.8. Note that each final topic score is multiplied by its weight to produce a quantity referred to as "quality points." The total quality points are summed and divided by the total weight (in this case, 12) to obtain a weighted average score of 2.71. On the surface, the suggestion to compute a weighted average might seem to contradict the discussion in previous chapters about the superiority of true score estimates based on the power law over those based on the average. The difference is that the earlier discussion assumes that all scores within a measurement topic represent the same dimension or dimensions that covary. In such situations, the scores from one assessment occasion to another are related in the sense that learning from one assessment to another will increase a student's true score on the topic. In the case of final scores on *different* measurement topics, the scores are independent. A student's score on the measurement topic *behavior* might have little or nothing to do with his score on the measurement topic *probability*. Each final topic score represents a true score estimate for a different dimension. When combining the scores for different topics, the only mathematical computation that is defensible is to average the scores in some weighted or unweighted fashion.

The use of the average also appears to contradict the previous discussion that scores should be rounded up or down to the nearest half-point value. Again, this situation is different in that we are combining scores for multiple topics as opposed to computing a final score for an individual topic. We might compare this situation to that of trying to summarize the heights of nine people (nine topics). This is commonly done using the numerical average. But anyone truly interested in the distribution of the heights of the nine people will want to know more than the average. In the next chapter we consider how to provide more information in the context of a report card.

Translating Scores to Traditional Grades

The average score for a set of academic and nonacademic topics could suffice as the final omnibus score for all topics addressed in a grading period. In such a system, the final "grade" for a student in a given class would be the student's weighted or unweighted average for the measurement topics addressed in the course. In the example in Figures 6.7 and 6.8, the student's summary score would be 2.71. However, a district or school that wishes to use the traditional A, B, C, D, and F grading protocol needs a translation, such as the following:

    3.00–4.00 = A
    2.50–2.99 = B
    2.00–2.49 = C
    1.50–1.99 = D
    Below 1.50 = F

Using this scheme, our sample student would receive a grade of B. Of course, this example is just that—an example. A district or school should construct its own scheme that best reflects its values regarding the meaning of grades. However, regardless of the scheme the district or school uses, it should realize that an overall letter grade is an artificial construct because the cutoff points for the various grades are arbitrary. This feature is one of the greatest weaknesses of using overall letter grades. Guskey (1996b) explains that the arbitrary nature of cutoff points is a built-in weakness in the system:

The cutoff between grade categories is always arbitrary and difficult to justify. If the scores for a grade of B range from 80–89 for example, a student with a score of 89 receives the same grade as the student with a score of 80 even though there is a 9-point difference in their scores. But the student with a score of 79—a 1-point difference—receives a grade of C because the cutoff for a B grade is 80. (p. 17)

Using a Conjunctive Approach

The system for weighting final topic scores and computing an overall grade as described is a compensatory system (Kifer, 1994) in that performance on one measurement topic can "compensate" for performance on another. To illustrate, assume that a student received the following scores on eight measurement topics:

Topic 1 = 1.5
Topic 2 = 2.5
Topic 3 = 2.5
Topic 4 = 4.0
Topic 5 = 1.5
Topic 6 = 1.5
Topic 7 = 1.5
Topic 8 = 4.0

The (unweighted) average score for this set is 2.38. Based on the descriptions of the half-point values in the complete scale, this average might be interpreted to indicate that the student knows the basics—the simpler details and processes— and has partial knowledge of the more complex ideas and processes. However, examining the eight topic scores shows that the student has a score of 1.5 for four of them. For half the topics, then, the student demonstrates partial knowledge only—even for simple details and processes. Obviously, the two high scores of 4.0 have provided an inflated view of the student's typical performance. This contrived but straightforward example illustrates the weakness of using a compensatory approach that produces a weighted or unweighted average. Sometimes the average score does not represent the typical score in a set because the scores in the set differ greatly.

An alternative to the compensatory approach is the conjunctive approach (Plake, Hambleton, & Jaeger, 1995). If a conjunctive approach is used to construct grades, one score does not "pull up" another. Rather, overall grades are determined by score patterns across the measurement topics. Figure 6.9 depicts two conjunctive systems out of many possibilities. The first system has a strong logic. To receive an *A*, all topic scores must be 3.0 or above; to receive a *B*, all topic scores must be 2.5 or above; and so on. Unfortunately, this system can be quite punitive

---

FIGURE 6.9
Two Possible Conjunctive Grading Systems

System 1

Grade	Score Pattern
A	No topic score below 3.0
B	No topic score below 2.5
C	No topic score below 2.0
D	No topic score below 1.5
F	Some topic scores below 1.5

System 2

Grade	Score Pattern
A	No topic score below 2.5 and the majority 3.0 or above
B	No topic score below 2.0 and the majority 2.5 or above
C	No topic score below 1.5 and the majority 2.0 or above
D	No topic score below 1.0 and the majority 1.5 or above
F	Some topic scores below 1.0 or the majority not above 1.5

---

in certain situations. For example, assume a student receives scores of 4.0 on all topics except one, for which she receives a score of 1.5. Using the first system, the student would receive a D. The second system is less harsh but still quite demanding. Using the second system the student would receive a C.

It is possible to construct variations of the second system that minimize the effects of an extremely low score. However, in the final analysis, constructing an overall grade simply cannot be done in a manner that is completely fair and interpretable. In Chapter 7 we consider some alternatives to overall grades.

Summary and Conclusions

Various techniques can be used for computing final scores for topics and translating these scores to grades. Computer software that is suited to the system described in this book has three characteristics. First, the software should allow teachers to easily enter multiple topic scores for an assessment. Second, it should provide for the most accurate estimate of a student's final score for each topic. Third, it should provide graphs depicting student progress. Compensatory and conjunctive systems are two ways to combine final topic scores to compute overall grades.

7

Report Cards and the Future of Standards-Based or Topic-Based Schooling

One of the messages in Chapter 6 is that a single letter grade is a less than optimal way to report student progress. Obviously, from the perspective of standards-based education, isolated overall letter grades (or overall percentage scores or even average rubric scores) are extremely deficient because they cannot provide the level of detailed feedback necessary to enhance student learning. This inherent weakness of overall or omnibus grades and scores has been recognized and discussed by a number of assessment experts (see Guskey, 1996b; Marzano, 2000; Stiggins, 1997). The basic premise of this chapter is that changing the format of report cards has the potential of altering K–12 education in the United States in dramatic and unprecedented ways. I believe that the biggest changes will occur when overall grades are not the norm. However, given how entrenched the overall letter grade is in American society, a school might wish to begin with a report card that provides this cultural icon along with detailed information on measurement topics.

Report Cards with Overall Grades and Topic Scores

The logical way to begin changing report cards is to create a report card that provides traditional letter grades along with final scores for each measurement topic addressed in a grading period. Such a report card is consistent with the analogy used in Chapter 6 regarding the average height of a group of people. The average is like the overall grade; but to have a complete picture of the distribution, you must know the heights of the individual people. The individual heights are like the individual topic scores.

Figure 7.1 shows a report card that provides both letter grades and scores for measurement topics. The sample is for 5th grade, but the format can easily be used for all grades, from kindergarten through grade 12. For the purposes of this discussion, we will assume that the school is departmentalized, with different teachers responsible for each subject. For this grading period, five subject areas have been addressed: language arts, mathematics, science, social studies, and art. Each teacher computed final topic scores using the techniques described in Chapters 5 and 6. These topic scores are reported as bar graphs within each subject area. Note that each subject area includes academic topics and the life skill topics *participation*, *work completion*, *behavior*, and *working in groups*.

At the top of the report card, traditional *A*, *B*, and *C* letter grades are reported for each subject area. These final grades were computed using either a compensatory or conjunctive approach, as described in Chapter 6. In effect, then, the top part of the report card is quite traditional. However, the detail provided by the topic scores for each subject area is not. Topic scores provide students and parents with a quick and easily interpreted view of performance on all the topics that contributed to the computation of the grade.

A report card like this could be accompanied by a traditional transcript that lists courses taken, credits earned (in the case of secondary schools), and an overall grade point average (GPA). Although such a system is not ideal, it does have two advantages. First, it provides a link to what people are familiar with because it reports overall grades and a traditional GPA. Second, it reports the final scores for all topics addressed within a grading period, thus providing far more information than the current version of the traditional report card. In addition, it provides a glimpse of what a more useful and valid report card might be like.

A Report Card with No Overall Grades

A report card with no overall grades would report exclusively on measurement topics. To illustrate, consider Figure 7.2, which again is a sample report card for grade 5. The report card has no overall *A*, *B*, or *C* letter grades, but it still organizes information by subject areas. For example, in mathematics, five academic topics have been addressed in this grading period: *number systems*, *estimation*, *addition/subtraction*, *multiplication/division*, and *ratio/proportion/percent*. The average score for these five topics is 2.80, reported in the top section of the report card. This is not translated into a letter grade.

FIGURE 7.1
Report Card with Grades and Topic Scores

		Subject Areas:	
Name:	Aida Haystead		
Address:	123 Some Street	Language Arts	B
City:	Anytown, CO 80000	Mathematics	B
Grade Level:	5	Science	D
Homeroom:	Ms. Becker	Social Studies	A
		Art	B

Language Arts

Reading:

Word Recognition and Vocabulary	3.5
Reading for Main Idea	2.5
Literary Analysis	3.0

Writing:

Language Conventions	4.0
Organization and Focus	2.0
Research and Technology	1.5
Evaluation and Revision	2.5
Writing Applications	1.0

Listening and Speaking:

Comprehension	3.0
Organization and Delivery	3.5
Analysis and Evaluation of Oral Media	2.0
Speaking Applications	2.0

Life Skills:

Participation	4.0
Work Completion	3.0
Behavior	4.0
Working in Groups	2.5

Mathematics

Number Systems	4.0
Estimation	2.5
Addition/Subtraction	3.5
Multiplication/Division	3.5
Ratio/Proportion/Percent	0.5

Life Skills:

Participation	4.0
Work Completion	2.5
Behavior	3.0
Working in Groups	2.0

FIGURE 7.1
Report Card with Grades and Topic Scores   *(continued)*

Science		
Matter and Energy	1.5	
Forces of Nature	2.5	
Diversity of Life	1.0	
Human Identity	2.0	
Interdependence of Life	0.5	
Life Skills:		
Participation	1.5	
Work Completion	2.0	
Behavior	3.0	
Working in Groups	1.0	
Social Studies		
The Influence of Culture	3.0	
Current Events	3.5	
Personal Responsibility	4.0	
Government Representation	4.0	
Human and Civil Rights	3.0	
Life Skills:		
Participation	4.0	
Work Completion	4.0	
Behavior	4.0	
Working in Groups	3.5	
Art		
Purposes of Art	1.5	
Art Skills	2.5	
Art and Culture	3.0	
Life Skills:		
Participation	2.5	
Work Completion	2.0	
Behavior	4.0	
Working in Groups	3.0	

Source: From *What Works in Schools: Translating Research into Action* by Robert J. Marzano, 2003, pp. 41–42. Copyright © 2003 ASCD. Adapted with permission.

FIGURE 7.2
Report Card with No Letter Grades

Name: Aida Haystead
Address: 123 Some Street
City: Anytown, CO 80000
Grade Level: 5
Homeroom: Ms. Becker

Subject Areas:

Language Arts	2.54	Participation	3.20
Mathematics	2.80	Work Completion	2.70
Science	1.50	Behavior	3.60
Social Studies	3.50	Working in Groups	2.40
Art	2.33		

Language Arts

Reading:

Word Recognition and Vocabulary	3.5
Reading for Main Idea	2.5
Literary Analysis	3.0

Writing:

Language Conventions	4.0
Organization and Focus	2.0
Research and Technology	1.5
Evaluation and Revision	2.5
Writing Applications	1.0

Listening and Speaking:

Comprehension	3.0
Organization and Delivery	3.5
Analysis and Evaluation of Oral Media	2.0
Speaking Applications	2.0

Life Skills:

Participation	4.0
Work Completion	3.0
Behavior	4.0
Working in Groups	2.5
Average for Language Arts	2.54

Mathematics

Number Systems	4.0
Estimation	2.5
Addition/Subtraction	3.5
Multiplication/Division	3.5
Ratio/Proportion/Percent	0.5

Life Skills:

Participation	4.0
Work Completion	2.5
Behavior	3.0
Working in Groups	2.0
Average for Mathematics	2.80

FIGURE 7.2
Report Card with No Letter Grades   *(continued)*

Science

Matter and Energy	1.5	
Forces of Nature	2.5	
Diversity of Life	1.0	
Human Identity	2.0	
Interdependence of Life	0.5	
Life Skills:		
Participation	1.5	
Work Completion	2.0	
Behavior	3.0	
Working in Groups	1.0	
Average for Science	1.50	

Social Studies

The Influence of Culture	3.0	
Current Events	3.5	
Personal Responsibility	4.0	
Government Representation	4.0	
Human and Civil Rights	3.0	
Life Skills:		
Participation	4.0	
Work Completion	4.0	
Behavior	4.0	
Working in Groups	3.5	
Average for Social Studies	3.50	

Art

Purposes of Art	1.5	
Art Skills	2.5	
Art and Culture	3.0	
Life Skills:		
Participation	2.5	
Work Completion	2.0	
Behavior	4.0	
Working in Groups	3.0	
Average for Art	2.33	

Source: From What Works in Schools: Translating Research into Action by Robert J. Marzano, 2003, pp. 41–42. Copyright © 2003 ASCD. Adapted with permission.

FIGURE 7.3
Traditional Subject Areas and Related Cross-Curricular Topics

Traditional Subject Area	Cross-Curricular Measurement Topics
Reading	Comprehension
Writing	Paragraph construction
Mathematics	Problem solving
Science	Hypothesis generation and testing

As before, each teacher has assigned final topic scores for the life skill areas *participation*, *work completion*, *behavior*, and *working in groups* within their subject areas. The average for these life skill topics across the five subject areas is reported at the top of the report card. Thus, in this example, the academic topics and the life skill topics are not combined in any way. This is an important distinction. The more traditional report card in Figure 7.1 reports on individual academic topics and life skill topics, but it combines all topics within a subject area into an overall grade. This practice mixes subject-specific academic topics with life skill topics. Although both types of topics are important, combining them makes little sense.

A variation on this theme is to identify some academic measurement topics that cut across subject areas. For example, assume that a district or school has identified the four measurement topics in Figure 7.3 as those to be addressed in a variety of subject areas. Each topic has a home in a traditional subject area. However, each represents an area of information and skill that is considered to be important enough that it will be reinforced in other subject areas as well. This does not mean that each topic must be addressed in every class every quarter. Rather, the district or school would probably identify selected nonmathematics classes in which problem solving would be addressed, and selected nonscience courses in which hypothesis generation and testing would be addressed, and so on. The final topic scores for these cross-curricular measurement topics would be aggregated across classes and reported as a category named something like *communication and reasoning* in the same manner as the life skill topics shown in Figure 7.2.

Of course, a report card like that depicted in Figure 7.2 would be accompanied by a transcript that reports cumulative progress over time. Figure 7.4 shows one version of such a transcript, depicting language arts only, for the sake of brevity. All subject areas would follow the same format. The columns represent

						Power Law Score
FIGURE 7.4 **Sample Transcript**						
Language Arts	**Q1**	**Q2**	**Q3**	**Q4**	**Average**	
Reading						
Word recognition and vocabulary	3.5	3.0	3.5	4.0	3.50	3.67
Reading for main idea	2.5	2.5	3.0	3.5	2.88	3.27
Literary analysis	3.0	3.0	3.5	3.5	3.25	3.49
Writing						
Language conventions	4.0	4.0			4.00	
Organization and focus	2.0	2.0	2.5	2.5	2.25	2.49
Research and technology	1.5		2.0		1.75	
Evaluation and revision	2.5	2.0	2.5	3.5	2.63	2.90
Writing applications	1.0	1.5	2.0	2.0	1.63	2.15
Listening and Speaking						
Comprehension	3.0	3.0	3.5	3.0	3.13	3.12
Organization and delivery	3.5			3.5	3.50	
Analysis and evaluation of oral media	2.0			2.0	2.00	
Speaking applications	2.0		2.5	3.0	2.50	2.86

quarters or grading periods (Q1, Q2, and so on) across a given year. Notice that not all measurement topics are addressed every quarter (this was discussed in Chapter 2). For those that are, the true score estimate based on the power law will probably be the best estimate. For those topics addressed once or twice throughout a year, the average will be the best estimate. In keeping with this principle, the last two columns of Figure 7.4 report the averages and the power law estimates.

Transforming the Culture of the District or School

Ultimately, to make these kinds of significant changes in report cards, a district or school must transform its culture from one in which individual teachers develop their own idiosyncratic methods of grading to a culture in which grading and reporting are uniform from teacher to teacher and subject to subject. As we have seen in the discussions in Chapters 2 through 6, using the system described in this book, teachers still have a great deal of freedom in how and when they assess students. However, the topics on which they report and the manner in which they present information on students' performance on those topics are uniform. Such uniformity is not accomplished quickly. Consequently, I recommend the following phases or sequence of events as a way to change from the current assessment and reporting system to the one recommended in this book.

Phase I

Have a vanguard team of teachers experiment with topic-based assessment and record keeping.

The first step to transforming the culture of a district or school is to recruit a small group of teachers who are willing to try out topic-based assessments and record keeping. This step should take about one semester and requires no substantial change; report cards do not have to be altered, districtwide or schoolwide measurement topics do not have to be identified, and common assessments do not have to be constructed. Rather, individual teachers on this vanguard team simply identify the academic and life skill topics they wish to address in a given grading period. They construct rubrics for each topic using the templates for the simplified or complete scale presented in Chapter 3. They design classroom assessments around their topics and administer them when appropriate. To keep track of student performance on the topics, they might use the method of mounting evidence presented in Chapter 5. To do so, they might construct a simple paper-and-pencil grade book, like the one shown in Figure 5.9. Another option is for these vanguard teachers to use inexpensive software that includes a grade book. To this end, I commonly recommend the single-user version of the Pinnacle Plus system produced by Excelsior Software. The grade book is free for individual users who wish to try out the system presented in this book. Information about the single-user version is available at http://www.excelsiorsoftware.com.

To illustrate how this first step might play out, assume that a 9th grade social studies teacher has volunteered to be part of the vanguard group for the second quarter of the school year. The teacher would identify a small set of measurement topics by considering the typical content she addresses during the quarter and then organizing that content into measurement topics, as described in Chapter 2. Given the general rule that she shouldn't try to keep track of too many academic topics (I recommend about five to seven academic topics per grading period), she might find that she cannot keep track of all the content she typically tries to cover. She might also find that some of the content organizes nicely into measurement topics, but other content does not. Consequently, she might decide to use a variation of the teacher-choice category described in Chapter 2. This category would include all the content that she considers important but that does not fit well into any one topic area. In addition to the academic topics, she would identify a few life skill topics she deems important.

With her personal topics identified, she would construct a scale for each topic using the general template found in Chapter 3, Figure 3.11. She would design and score assessments in keeping with the recommendations in Chapters 3 and 4, and compute final topic scores in keeping with the suggestions in Chapters 5 and 6.

The reason for using a vanguard group is to have volunteer teachers obtain some experience with the new system of assessment and grading. My experience has been that vanguard groups are a critical step in transforming the culture of a school. They will have credibility with their peers as to the viability of the new assessment and grading system. I have also found that, for the most part, teachers who take part in a vanguard group become strong advocates for the new system. They see the inherent weaknesses in the traditional system and the potential of the new system.

Phase II

Identify the measurement topics that will be used throughout the district or school, the software that will be used to keep track of student performance on the topics, and the grading system that will be used.

Assuming that the vanguard group has had a positive experience, the next step is to identify measurement topics. Ideally, this should be done at the district level and should take about one to one and one-half years, beginning at the end of Phase I. During Phase II, a small group of subject matter specialists meets frequently to construct first drafts of the measurement topics for each subject area at each grade level. In keeping with the discussion in Chapter 2, I recommend that measurement topics be designed for kindergarten through grade 9 and possibly through grade 10—whatever grade level represents the end point for teaching content that every student should master, regardless of their plans after high school. These measurement topics should be considered general literacy topics in that they represent information and skill considered to be important for successful participation in society at large. Above grade 9 (or 10), different measurement topics should be identified for specialized courses and advanced courses that go beyond the basic measurement topics.

In all cases, the specialists should identify no more than 20 measurement topics within a given subject area for a given year. Ideally the number of measurement topics should be closer to 15, and within these topics a relatively few covarying elements should be identified—no more than five elements per topic and ideally about three. In addition to academic topics, a small set of life skill topics should be identified. I recommend no more than five. These topics might be the same from kindergarten through grade 12, although the specific covarying elements within each topic at the higher grades would be different from those at the lower grades. All academic topics should be stated in terms of the complete nine-point scale first depicted in Chapter 3, Figure 3.11. (See also Figure 3.14 for an example of the complete nine-point scale written for a specific measurement topic.) Life skill topics might be stated in the simplified five-point scale. (See Figure 4.10 for examples of simplified five-point scales written for specific life skill topics.) Once first drafts of academic and life skill topics have been designed, they should be reviewed by teachers and stakeholders who were not involved in the design process. The information from these reviews should be used to construct second drafts of topics.

Concurrent with the execution of Phase II, a group of knowledgeable individuals from the district should identify the computer software that will be used to keep track of student performance on the topics. Ideally, vanguard teachers have had an opportunity to try out an inexpensive version of the software during Phase I. The software that is selected should be able to perform the operations described in Chapter 6, such as the following:

• Computing an estimated final true score based on the power function and the average

• Mathematically determining which estimate of the true score best fits the data

• Allowing for the differential weighting of topics

• Allowing for multiple ways of aggregating topics into higher-level categories (standards, strands, and the like)

The final activity of Phase II is to determine the grading system that will be used. This chapter has presented two systems—one that involves overall letter grades as well as scores for academic and life skill measurement topics, and one that does not involve overall letter grades but organizes measurement topics into subject matter categories. There are probably many other ways to aggregate and report measurement topics. Choosing an option should be done during Phase II, allowing for proper vetting and input from relevant stakeholders.

Phase III

Implement the system in stages.

Once Phases I and II are complete, the topic-based record-keeping and reporting system that has been designed should be implemented in stages. As noted, Phases I and II should take one and one-half to two years to complete. Thus, the new record-keeping and reporting system is not actually implemented until about the third year of the effort. This allows time to identify and fix "bugs" and time for teachers and other stakeholders to have input into the design of the system.

A case can be made that the system, once designed, should be implemented throughout the district. A change this drastic is never easy. Consequently, one might just as well do it in one fell swoop. However, it is also true that the system can be implemented in stages. Probably the part of the K–12 system that will be the least resistant to the new record-keeping and reporting system will be the elementary schools. After one year of implementation in the elementary schools, the system can be implemented in the middle schools; and one year after that, the system can be implemented in the high schools. During this staged implementation, adjustments and additions to the system should be made. For example, during Phase III, the district might develop end-of-quarter assessments or common assessments to be used by teachers along with their formative classroom assessments. In all, then, the entire system can be implemented in three years using a staged approach after the completion of Phases I and II.

From Transforming the Culture to Transforming Education

If implemented correctly, the three phases will dramatically change the culture of K–12 education from one that has little formative data with which to identify student strengths and weaknesses to one that is data-rich. Students who are having difficulty with a particular measurement topic can be identified early in their academic careers and provided with help where needed. A data-rich system would dramatically lower the probability that students could progress through the grade levels with severe weaknesses in key areas. Such an accomplishment is noteworthy.

However, a well-articulated and well-implemented topic-based system of record keeping and reporting has the potential to effect changes that are even more dramatic. Specifically, it can change education into a system in which learning is constant and time is variable, as opposed to the current system in which learning is variable and time is constant. This revolutionary concept has been advocated and discussed by many individuals with a number of variations on the theme (e.g., Bloom, 1976; Boyer, 1983, 1995; Goodlad, 1984; Guskey, 1980, 1985, 1987; Spady 1988, 1992, 1994, 1995). According to J. Ronald Gentile and James Lalley (2003), the genesis of the various manifestations of the concept can be traced to the work of John Carroll (1963, 1989). The Carroll model can be represented by the following formula:

$$\text{Amount of learning} \quad = \quad \frac{\text{Time actually spent}}{\text{Time needed to learn}}$$

According to this formula, the amount any student learns relative to a given measurement topic is a function of the time the student actually spends learning the topic and the time needed to learn the topic. If a student has spent 5 hours on a topic but needs 10 hours, then she has not learned the topic well. This fact has some important implications for the discussion in Chapter 2 regarding the amount of time estimated to be necessary to learn the content in the national and state standards. Given the estimate that 71 percent more instructional time than is now available is needed to teach the content in the national and state standards, there is little chance that U.S. students will learn the content in the standards well. Hence, there is a need to dramatically cut the amount of content that teachers are expected to teach and students are expected to learn.

Carroll's formula discloses another interesting issue—the problem created by the fact that students require differing amounts of time to learn content. Specifically, a good deal of research indicates that students enter school with vastly different amounts of academic background knowledge for specific subject areas (for a discussion, see Marzano, 2004b). Those students who have a great deal of academic background knowledge for a given subject area can move through the content relatively quickly; those who do not have much background knowledge require a great deal more time.

At a basic level, Carroll's model implies that an optimal educational system would be one in which students could take as much or as little time as is necessary to learn the content of the measurement topics. However, at least two conventions that are engrained in our current system work against the realization of Carroll's model—grade levels and credits.

The concept of grade levels is an essential part of what David Tyack and William Tobin (1994) refer to as the "grammar" of U.S. education—the notion that schools should be organized by grade levels is so engrained in the culture that it is rarely if ever challenged. Arguably, grade levels organized by student age became entrenched in U.S. education at the beginning of the 20th century in part because the method represented a straightforward and intuitively appealing way to categorize students at a time when public education expanded dramatically. As Diane Ravitch (1983) notes,

> With each passing decade, American youth went to school for a longer portion of the year and for a longer period of their lives. From 1870 to 1940, while the population tripled, school enrollment rates soared. Students in secondary schools increased by a multiple of almost 90, from eighty thousand in 1870 to 7 million in 1940. . . . The rise in educational participation was due to economic and social factors. In 1900, most male workers were either farmers or laborers. As the century advanced, fewer men worked in these occupations, while more men held white-collar occupations and skilled blue-collar jobs. (pp. 9–10)

Once schools established grade levels, society at large accepted the practice as an essential ingredient of effective education. However, by definition, grade levels work against students progressing through content at their own pace. Regardless of their understanding of and skill at the content addressed at a given grade, all students, with some rare exceptions, are moved through the system at exactly the same pace. Time in school is constant; learning is greatly varied.

Another convention that works against the realization of Carroll's model is the use of credits as the basic indicator of progress within a subject area at the secondary level. Students must spend a specific amount of time in a course to receive credit for the course. A demonstration of only minimum competence (a grade of D) is required. Again, time is constant and learning is greatly varied. Credits can be traced back some 100 years, when, in 1906, Henry S. Smith, the president of the Carnegie Foundation for the Advancement of Teaching, defined a *unit* as a course of five periods weekly throughout an academic year (Tyack & Tobin, 1994). In his book *High School: A Report on Secondary Education in America*, Ernest Boyer (1983) explains that the credit approach has spawned a virtual "logjam" (p. 237) in terms of allowing students to progress through subject areas at their own pace.

Although it might not be obvious, a district organized around measurement topics using classroom-based formative assessments has the potential of overriding the convention of traditional grade levels in the earlier years and the convention of credits at the high school level. In fact, a topic-based system highlights the illogical nature of grades and credits. To illustrate, consider a 7th grade student in a school district using a topic-based approach. In mathematics the student might be quite capable of addressing the 8th grade topics. Forcing the student to work on the 7th grade mathematics topics will most likely serve to bore the student with content already mastered. However, the 7th grade language arts topics might be beyond the student's current level of expertise. In this subject area she is better suited to work on the 6th grade topics. Working on the 7th grade language arts topics will most likely frustrate the student with content that is too complex for her developmental level. With some reorganizing of schedules and resources, a topic-based system as described in this book could alleviate these issues. More specifically, a system that implements Carroll's model necessarily will be *porous*.

In a completely porous system a student could work at any level in any subject area. The system would be totally porous in that (theoretically) a student could be working on the 2nd grade level in one subject area and the 10th grade level in another. In fact, in such a system, the term *grade level* would most probably be dropped in favor of the more generic term *level*. Although such a system would be ideal, it is probably difficult if not impossible to implement in most districts as they are currently designed. High school campuses are situated far from middle school campuses, which are situated far from elementary school campuses. In effect, the logistics of most districts do not allow for a totally porous K–12 approach. There are other viable options, however.

In his book *A Place Called School*, John Goodlad (1984) proposed that schools should be organized in three tiers, each representing four grade levels. In other works (Marzano & Kendall, 1996), I have recommended four tiers: K–2, 3–5, 6–8, and 9–12. Each tier would be porous. That is, a student in 5th grade could easily move up to the 6th grade topics for mathematics and down to the 3rd grade level for language arts. Teachers within a tier would address different grade-level topics. For example, within the 3–5 tier, some teachers would address the 3rd grade mathematics topics, others would address the 4th grade topics, and still others the 5th grade topics. Of course, mathematics instruction would have to be scheduled at the same time within a tier to allow students to move up or down as needed. The same is true for other subject areas. As soon as students demonstrated mastery of the topics at one level, they would move on to the next. Thus, students would not necessarily spend an entire year at a particular level. Student who demonstrated that they could move through the topics at a given level in six months would move on to the next level. Likewise, students requiring more than one year to demonstrate competence on the topics at a given level would stay at that level until they attained competence.

A logical question is, what happens to students in the second tier (grades 3–5) who should be working on 2nd grade topics or 6th grade topics within a given subject area? This is most easily handled by organizing students who are below or above tier expectations into separate homogeneous groups. Students in the below-tier group would work on those topics on which they are "behind" with the goal of raising their competence to the lowest level of the regular tier as quickly as possible. Students who operate beyond tier expectations for a given subject area would be grouped together so that they might work on advanced topics. Thus they would enter the next tier already ahead of the minimum-level expectations for that tier. In effect, up through the third tier, each tier would have vehicles in place for those students who enter the tier below the base levels for a given subject area, as well as for those who enter beyond the expectations for the terminal level.

For high school students, the concept of certificates of initial mastery and advanced mastery as described in Chapter 2 might be used. A certificate of initial mastery in mathematics, for example, would indicate that the student had mastered the general mathematics content important for participation in society. A student wishing to receive a certificate of advanced mastery in mathematics would take courses that provide instruction and validation in the advanced mathematics topics. Students would graduate from high school with certificates of initial mastery in some subject areas and certificates of advanced mastery in others, depending on their interests and motivation. To graduate, all students would be required to attain a certificate of initial mastery for certain core subject areas such as mathematics, reading, writing, and science (or whatever the district identified as core areas). Other than the requirements in the core areas, students would be free to select those areas in which they wish to excel as demonstrated by a certificate of advanced mastery.

Although the system described here is not without some logistical and resource problems, I firmly believe these problems are all solvable within the current system and the resources available to that system. In other words, the system described can be implemented immediately, assuming a district has done the requisite work on measurement topics and formative assessments described in this book.

Where Is This Being Done?

Many times scenarios such as that articulated here are hypothetical only. They inspire us but also instill a nagging doubt that the vision they portray is out of our reach in the near future, as evidenced by the fact that no one is currently implementing the system. In this case, a more promising situation exists. A small but growing group of districts have implemented the vision. Many of those districts are involved in the Reinventing Schools Coalition, or RISC, and use the Reinventing Schools Model. As described by Rick Schreiber and Wendy Battino (2002) in *A Guide to Reinventing Schools*, Chugach School District in south-central Alaska is the genesis of the Reinventing Schools Model. Chugach School District includes most of the Prince William Sound coastline and islands, and its students are scattered throughout 22,000 square miles. As a direct consequence of its reform efforts and the leadership of Superintendent Richard DeLorenzo, Chugach became the first district to be awarded the New American High School Award and among the first three education organizations to win the prestigious Malcolm Baldrige Excellence Award.

Chugach began its comprehensive restructuring efforts in 1994 by seeking input from all the relevant stakeholders in the system, including parents, students, teachers, administrators, and representatives from the business community and the community at large. Based on this input, Chugach identified 10 areas of standards and specific levels of understanding and performance in each area. The 10 areas are (1) mathematics, (2) science, (3) technology, (4) reading, (5) writing, (6) social studies, (7) service learning, (8) career development, (9) cultural awareness, and (10) personal/social/health development. The stakeholders understood and embraced these areas because they were involved in identifying and designing them. As Schreiber and Battino (2002) note, "Teachers, parents, students, and community members are aware of student educational goals because they helped to create the standards" (p. ix). Within the Chugach system, students progress through various levels as opposed to grades. Competence for a given level is demonstrated by teacher-designed classroom assessments as well as district-designed common assessments.

As one would expect, given that Chugach won the coveted Baldrige award, it has demonstrated the positive effects of its system on student achievement. To illustrate, consider Figure 7.5, which shows national percentile scores from the

---

FIGURE 7.5
National Percentile Scores for Chugach Students

School Year	Total Reading	Total Language	Total Math	Total Spelling
1994–95	28	26	36	22
1995–96	43	44	54	32
1996–97	56	50	58	35
1997–98	63	60	66	46
1998–99	71	72	78	65

Source: From *A Guide to Reinventing Schools* by R. Schreiber & W. Battino, 2002, Chugach, AK: Reinventing Schools Coalition.

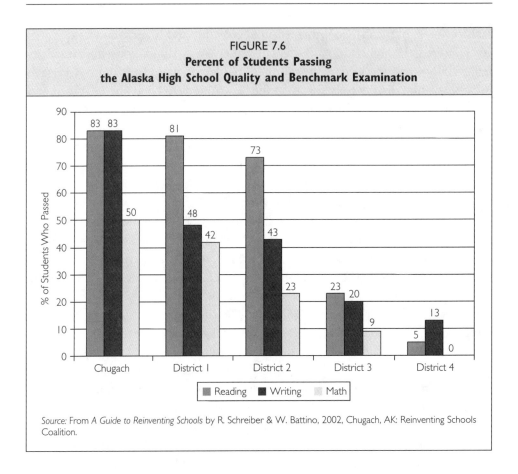

FIGURE 7.6
**Percent of Students Passing
the Alaska High School Quality and Benchmark Examination**

Source: From *A Guide to Reinventing Schools* by R. Schreiber & W. Battino, 2002, Chugach, AK: Reinventing Schools Coalition.

California Achievement Test (CAT) beginning in 1994–95, when the system was initiated. As the figure shows, the percentile ranks for Chugach students increased consistently over a five-year period in all four subject areas. According to Schreiber and Battino (2002), "Current levels and trends indicate that CSD [Chugach] students are improving at a higher rate than those in competitive districts" (p. 320).

Indeed, Chugach compares quite favorably to other districts in Alaska. To illustrate, consider Figure 7.6, which shows the percentage of students in Chugach and four other districts who passed the 2000 Alaska High School Quality and Benchmark Examination in reading, writing, and mathematics. Chugach had higher percentages of students passing the examination in all three areas even though two of the comparison districts had strong advantages over Chugach in terms of the socioeconomic makeup of their students.

Perhaps the most impressive achievement data Chugach can offer are from a third-party evaluation regarding the efforts of other school districts to replicate the Chugach model (see Coladarci, Smith, & Whiteley, 2005). Specifically, 15 school districts were involved in efforts to reform their systems using the RISC approach to change and standards-based education. The study examined the relationship between the extent to which the 15 districts adhered to the RISC protocols and achievement on the Alaska High School Qualifying and Benchmark Examination. Strong positive correlations between adherence to RISC protocols and achievement on the Alaska state assessment were found for reading, writing, and mathematics (.57, .33, and .54, respectively).

In summary, Chugach School District and districts trying to emulate its efforts through involvement in the Reinventing Schools Coalition have shown that a standards-based system that allows students to progress freely through various levels of achievement as demonstrated by performance on classroom-based assessment not only is viable but also has a demonstrated positive impact on students' academic achievement.

Conclusions

This book has provided a detailed description of an approach to standards-based, or topic-based, formative classroom assessment that has the potential to dramatically enhance student achievement because of the specificity and timeliness of feedback. The approach also has the potential to transform education from the current system in which students progress through grade levels based on time spent in school to a system in which students progress at their own individual rates as a consequence of demonstrated competence in content knowledge. I firmly believe that this change would raise K–12 education to a level of effectiveness and efficiency never before seen in its history. I also believe that the level of detail provided in this book equips educators with all the tools they need to bring about that more effective and efficient system.

Technical Notes

Technical Note 1.1

"Most effective" versus "least effective" teachers were identified by ranking them in terms of gains in student achievement and then organizing the rank order into five categories, or quintiles. "Most effective" teachers were defined as those in the highest category (Quintile 1); "least effective" teachers were defined as those in the lowest category (Quintile 5). For a technical discussion, see Haycock (1998); Sanders and Horn (1994); and Wright, Horn, and Sanders (1997).

Technical Note 1.2

The term *effect size* refers to a number of indices that quantify the strength of relationship between an independent variable and a dependent variable or between a predictor variable and a predicted variable. These indices include r (the bivariate correlation coefficient), R (the multiple correlation coefficient), and PV (the percentage of variance accounted for). As used in this book, the general term *effect size* refers to what is arguably the most common effect size, the *standardized mean difference*, popularized by Glass (1976). It is the difference between experimental and control means divided by an estimate of the population standard deviation—hence the name *standardized mean difference*.

$$\text{standardized mean difference effect size} = \frac{\text{mean of experimental group minus mean of control group}}{\text{estimate of population standard deviation}}$$

To illustrate how the standardized mean difference (henceforth referred to as *effect size*) is calculated and interpreted, assume that the achievement mean of a school with a given characteristic is 90 on a test, and the mean of a school that does not possess this characteristic is 80. Also assume that the population standard deviation is 10. The effect would be

$$\text{effect size} = \frac{90 - 80}{10} = 10$$

This effect size can be interpreted in the following way: The mean of the group with the characteristic (the experimental group) is one standard deviation greater than the mean of the group without the characteristic (the control group). Assuming that the characteristic in question is not simply a function of chance and that the two groups are equal on all characteristics other than the one in question, one might infer that the characteristic possessed by the experimental group raises the average score of students in a school by one standard deviation. In other words, the effect size is expressed in "z score" form. This allows for an interpretation in terms of percentile gain.

Percentile gain is the expected gain (or loss) in percentile points of a student at the 50th percentile in the experimental group as compared to a student at the 50th percentile in the control group. To illustrate, given an effect size of 1.0, one can infer that a student with a score at the mean in the experimental group will be at about the 84th percentile in the control group. This is so because distribution theory tells us that a z score of 1.0 is at the 84.134th percentile point of the standard normal distribution. Thus the student at the 50th percentile in the experimental group is one standard deviation above the mean in the control group.

Technical Note 1.3

To construct Figure 1.1, the effect size of .70 reported by Black and Wiliam (1998) was translated to a bivariate correlation coefficient using the formula r = effect size/(effect size^2+4)^.5. This resulted in an r of .33. This allows one to predict the z score in a dependent variable given a specific increase in the z score of an independent variable. The equation for this prediction is

$$z'_y = r_{xy} z_{xy}$$

Described in words, this equation states that the predicted z score or standard score on variable y (indicated by the apostrophe) is equal to the correlation between x and y multiplied by the z score on x. As Magnusson (1966) notes:

When we know an individual's observed standard score on x (z_x) and the correlation coefficient for the relationship between scores on the x-distribution and scores on the y-distribution, we can obtain the best possible prediction of the individual's standard score on y by multiplying z_x by the correlation coefficient. (p. 39)

To compute the gain in student achievement associated with a gain in teacher effectiveness at formative assessment depicted in the upper part of Figure 1.1, the assumption was made that effectiveness at formative assessment was the independent variable and student achievement was the dependent variable. It was also assumed that a given student was at the 50th percentile in achievement, and a given teacher was at the 50th percentile in effectiveness at formative assessment. Thus, the independent and dependent variables both have a z score of 0. However, if the teacher increased her effectiveness at formative effectiveness by one standard deviation, her z score would increase to 1.0, placing her at about the 84th percentile on the distribution of use of formative assessment. Using the formula above, one would predict the student's z score to increase to .33 (i.e., $z'_y = r_{xy} z_x = (.33)(1.0) = .33$). Consulting the standard normal distribution, a z score of .33 translates to a percentile gain (in this context) of 13 points. To compute the gain in student achievement depicted in the lower part of Figure 1.1, the same assumptions were made. However, in this case the assumption was made that the teacher increased her effectiveness at formative assessment by 2.33 standard deviations, placing her at the 99th percentile. Using the formula above, one would predict the student's z score to increase to .769 (i.e., $z'_y = r_{xy} z_x = [.33][2.33] = .769$). Consulting the standard normal distribution, a z score of .769 translates to a percentile gain of 28 points.

Technical Note 1.4

The Bangert-Drowns, Kulik, and Kulik (1991) meta-analysis extrapolates the effect size for formative assessments over a 15-week period, assuming a nonlinear relationship between student achievement and the number of assessments administered. They provide a graph representing their nonlinear extrapolation. Using their graph, the values depicted in Figure 1.3 were imputed.

Technical Note 2.1

In a series of articles, John Hattie (Hattie, 1984, 1985; Hattie et al., 1996) identified a number of misconceptions regarding the construct of unidimensionality. He explains:

> A fundamental assumption of test theory is that a score can only have meaning if the set of items measures only one attribute or dimension. If the measurement instrument

is composed of items that measure different dimensions, then it is difficult to interpret the total score from a set of items, to make psychological sense when relating variables, or to interpret individual differences. Despite the importance of this assumption to all testing models, there have been few systematic attempts to investigate this assumption and, until recently, little success at providing a defensible procedure to assess the claim of unidimensionality. (Hattie et al., 1996, p. 1)

In his 1984 study, Hattie examined 87 indices of unidimensionality and concluded that "almost all of the indices . . . were not effective" (p. 75). As a result of these findings regarding indices of unidimensionality, Hattie ultimately questioned the viability of unidimensionality as an ideal for test development: "Finally, it must be considered that it may be unrealistic to search for indices of unidimensionality or sets of unidimensional items" (1985, p. 159). Hattie notes that items and indices based on item responses in themselves might not adequately determine if a set of items is unidimensional because individual examinees will address items in different ways: "Much recent research has indicated that the same set of test items may be attacked by persons using different cognitive strategies" (1985, p. 159). Ultimately, Hattie concedes that judgment must enter into the determination of a test's unidimensionality:

> Further, it may be that an act of judgment and not an index is required. Kelly (1942) argued that embodied in such concepts as unidimensionality is a belief or point of view of the investigator such that an act of judgment is demanded when a researcher asserts that items measure the same thing. Thus, not only may it be possible to recognize by inspection whether one test appears to be unidimensional when compared to another, but also even if there is an index, then judgment must still be used. (1985, p. 159)

Although Hattie does not address the concept of a measurement topic as articulated in Chapter 2, his comments are germane in that unidimensionality or covariance of items is in part a function of how content is approached instructionally. Thus, curriculum specialists within a district must be involved in the identification and articulation of unidimensional constructs or constructs with covarying elements.

Technical Note 2.2

As used in the discussion in Chapter 2, *covariance* loosely refers to a relationship in which ability in one trait or dimension is related to ability in another trait or dimension, such that as one increases, so does the other. At a more technical and statistical level, *covariance* is defined as the ratio of the sum of the cross-products of the deviation scores for two variables divided by the number of pairs of observations:

$$covariance = \frac{Summation(y_i - mean\ y)(x_i - mean\ x)}{n}$$

where y_i refers to the score of student i on the y variable (or predicted or dependent variable) and x_i refers to the score of student i on the x variable (or predictor or independent variable). The terms in parentheses in the numerator are referred to as *deviation scores*, or the distance between each observed score and the mean of the observed distribution. When the covariance for a set of scores is divided by the product of the standard deviation of the independent or predictor variable and the dependent or predicted variable, one has the bivariate correlation coefficient (Cohen, Cohen, West, & Aiken, 2003, p. 29). That is,

$$r_{yx} = \frac{covariance_{yx}}{(sd_y)(sd_x)}$$

Technical Note 3.1

The concept of *true score* has its roots in classical test theory (CTT) as opposed to item response theory (IRT). Hambleton, Swaminathan, and Rogers (1991) explain true score in the following way: "What do we mean by ability? In the classical test theory framework, the notion of ability is expressed by the true score, which is defined as 'the expected value of observed performance on the test of interest' " (p. 2). Lord (1959) explains that *true score* is "frequently defined as the average of the scores that an examinee would make on all possible parallel tests if he did not change during the testing process" (p. 473). Gulliksen (1950) defines *true score* for a given student as "the limit that the average of his scores on a number of tests approaches, as the number of parallel tests . . . increases without limit" (p. 28). Finally, Magnusson (1966) describes *true score* in the following way: "true score which can be predicted with complete certainty from the latent continuum is the same for every individual from one parallel test to another" (p. 63).

One implication of this definition is that true score is tied to a specific test. Note that each definition defines *true score* in the context of a specific test or parallel tests. This circumscribes the interpretation of true score. As Hambleton and colleagues (1991) explain, "An examinee's ability is defined only in terms of a particular test. When the test is 'hard,' the examinee will appear to have ability; when the test is 'easy,' the examinee will appear to have higher ability" (p. 2). IRT models speak in terms of *latent traits* as opposed to true scores. The latent trait continuum is not defined in terms of a specific test. Rather, it is defined in terms of hypothetical distribution of scores for the basic dimension measured by the test.

Technical Note 3.2

There are many IRT models, yet all share common characteristics. As Embretson and Reise (2000) explain, "All IRT-based scoring strategies attempt to estimate an examinee's location on a latent-trait continuum by using an examinee's pattern of item responses in conjunction with estimated item parameters" (p. 158). One of the first and most basic IRT models is the Rasch model, named after originator Georg Rasch (1960). Rasch articulated a number of models, but the one most commonly associated with his name uses the simple difference between a person's trait score (T) and an item's level of difficulty (D):

$$p(X_{is} = 1 \mid T_s, D_i) = \frac{\exp(T_s - D_i)}{1 + \exp(T_s - D_i)}$$

where:

- T_s is the trait score for person s
- D_i is the difficulty of item i
- $p(X_{is} = 1 \mid T_s, D_i)$ is read as the probability that a response (X) for person s on item i is correct (1) given a specific trait score (T) for person s and a given difficulty level D for item i
- $\exp(T_s - D_i)$ indicates to take the natural antilog of the difference between the person's trait score and the item difficulty. This quantity may also be written $\varepsilon^{(T_s - D_i)}$ (see Embretson & Reise, 2000, p. 50).

In words, this formula indicates that the probability of a person with a given trait score answering correctly a specific item with a given difficulty level is equal to ε (the Napierian base, approximately 2.7183) raised to the power of the person's trait score minus the item difficulty divided by 1 plus ε raised to the power of the person's trait score minus the item difficulty. For each item on a test, *item response curves* for a range of trait scores are computed using a model formula like the one here. Item response curves display the probability of answering an item correctly or *endorsing* the item for each potential trait score. Commonly, trait scores and item difficulties are expressed on a scale that ranges from −3.0 to +3.0. Even though these metrics resemble z scores, they are not the same. In general, to compute a person's trait score on a given test, the probability of a range of trait scores is computed for an individual's pattern of responses using the item response curves for the items. The trait score that has the highest computed probability is considered the trait score for the person as evidenced by the test. These trait scores are commonly transformed to another metric (e.g., one that ranges from 0 to 1,000) for ease of interpretation.

Technical Note 3.3

The concept of the *normal distribution* has had a profound effect on educational practice. The mathematical equation for the normal distribution was formulated by Abraham de Moivre (1667–1754) as early as 1733; however, its importance was articulated by mathematicians Pierre Simon de Laplace (1749–1827) and Carl Friedrich Gauss (1777–1855). So compelling were Gauss's writings about the normal distribution that today he is commonly considered the father of the normal distribution. In fact, it is sometimes referred to as the "Gaussian distribution."

What is referred to as the normal distribution is actually a family of distributions that are a function of two parameters, the mean of the distribution and the variance. Distributions with relatively large variances are flat in shape. Distributions with relatively small variances are peaked in shape. Regardless of these parameters, all distributions in the family of normal distribution share common characteristics, perhaps the most recognizable of which is that they have one hump in the middle and are symmetrical around the mean, as depicted in Figure 3.4. What is most frequently referred to as the *normal distribution* is that member of the family of distributions for which raw scores are expressed in z score form. This distribution is referred to as the *unit normal distribution*. Using the unit normal distribution, most statistics textbooks report a table of the proportions of scores expected to fall between the mean and a range of scores expressed in z score form.

One of the most compelling aspects of the normal distribution is that many characteristics are well described by it. For example, Geoffrey Harrison, Joseph Weiner, James Tanner, and N.A. Barnicot (1964) have reported that the height in inches of young Englishmen called upon for military service in 1939 followed a normal distribution. Similarly, Cyril Burt (1957) reported that IQ scores of 2,835 children randomly selected from London schools followed a normal distribution. In short, it is commonly assumed that randomly selected scores on any trait will approximate a normal distribution. Measurement theory from the early 20th century to the present has used the unit normal distribution as a critical point of reference.

Technical Note 3.4

In his article "Measurement 101: Some Fundamentals Revisited," David Frisbie (2005) identifies a series of misconceptions regarding the nature and application of measurement theory. For the most part, he deals with two measurement concepts that arguably are the basics of measurement theory: validity and reliability. About validity he notes that the technical literature clearly states "that validity is not about instruments themselves, but it is about score interpretation and uses" (p. 22). Consequently, it is inaccurate to talk about the validity of a test per se. This fact notwithstanding, he cites numerous examples of the misuse of the concept of validity:

> Here are some examples from a variety of sources that demonstrate the kind of misunderstanding about validity I'm talking about:
>
> 1. ". . . the term 'screening reading assessment' means an assessment that is valid . . . and based on scientifically based reading research; . . . " (NCLB Act of 2002, Public Law 107-110)
> 2. ". . . you can help ensure that the test will be valid and equitable for all students." (From an examiner's manual for a statewide assessment program, 2005)
> 3. "Evidence of test validity . . . should be made publicly available." (From a major publication of a prominent testing organization, 2002)
> 4. "In the assessment realm, this is referred to as the validity of the test." (From an introductory assessment textbook, 2005)
> 5. "[Test name] has proven itself in use for more than 50 years as a . . . valid test. . . ." (From web site of a prominent test publisher, 2005)
> 6. "Such efforts represent the cornerstone of test validity." (From the technical manual of a prominent achievement test, 2003). (p. 22)

Frisbie (2005) offers the same basic conclusions about the concept of reliability: "It seems that a similar statement needs to be made about reliability, and with the same rigor and emphasis. That is, reliability is not about an instrument per se. . . . Reliability is a property of a set of scores, not of the assessments that produce the scores" (p. 25). Again, he offers examples of apparent misconceptions about the concept of reliability:

> 1. "Such assessments shall be used for purposes for which such assessments are . . . reliable. . . ." (NCLB Act of 2002 Public Law 107-110)
> 2. "These are used to study . . . the reliability of assessment." (Standards and Assessments Peer Review Guidance, NCLB, 2004)
> 3. "The contractor will perform psychometric analyses to monitor the content, construct validity and reliability of the tests." (From RFP from a third state education department, 2003)
> 4. "The vendor must document that the proposed test(s) are reliable, valid, and free from bias. . . . In general, the test score issued for individual students in a single subject area should have a test reliability coefficient of approximately 0.85 or higher." (From an RFP from a fourth state department of education, 2003)
> 5. "Because test reliability is greatly influenced by the number of items in a test. . . ." (From a technical manual of a prominent achievement test battery, 2002) (pp. 25–26)

The comments of Frisbie regarding validity and reliability relate directly to the discussion in Chapter 3 regarding the measurement scale proposed for scoring classroom assessments. That scale focuses on the teacher's interpretation of student responses as opposed to an assessment considered in isolation.

Technical Note 5.1

Throughout the text the power function or "power law" is used as the mathematical model of choice to represent learning over time. The basic equation for the power function is $y = at^b$ where y is the score on a particular assessment, t is time at which the assessment was administered, and a and b are constants. As described in Chapters 3, 5, and 6, many psychologists assert that the power law is ubiquitous (Newell & Rosenbloom, 1981) and consequently a desirable function with which to model true score change over time.

Although the power function is the model used in this book to describe learning over time, it certainly is not the only possible model of true score development. In fact, there is a set of potential candidates. To illustrate, assume that y represents an individual's score for a particular topic or trait, and t represents the time that the score was obtained. Assuming that learning occurs over time, the following are all viable candidates to model that learning: (1) a linear function, (2) an exponential function, (3) a logarithmic function, (4) a quadratic function, and (5) a "pseudo-power function" derived by transforming independent and dependent variables into their natural log, computing a linear function, and then transforming the predicted scores back to their original metric. To examine the viability of these functions, consider Figure TN5.1A. The first row contains the original set of observed scores. The second row contains the predicted scores obtained by applying the power function to the observed data and then computing the predicted scores. The remaining rows contain the predicted scores produced by applying their respective functions. Inspection of Figure TN5.1A indicates that the predicted scores vary from each other and the original scores to greater and lesser degrees.

One way to judge the relative effectiveness of the various functions that might be used to model true score development is to examine the percentage of variance they account for. This is shown in Figure TN5.1B. All functions except for the logarithmic function account for more than 90 percent of the variance in the observed scores. The quadratic function explains the most variance.

In summary, although the power function is used in this text in discussions regarding modeling learning over time, a variety of viable functions can be used.

FIGURE TN5.1A Functions for Modeling Learning over Time					
Original Score	I	1.50	1.50	2.00	2.50
Power	.984	1.413	1.747	2.031	2.282
Linear	1.00	1.350	1.700	2.050	2.400
Exponential	1.062	1.313	1.623	2.006	2.480
Logarithmic	.903	1.480	1.817	2.057	2.243
Quadratic	1.071	1.315	1.629	2.014	2.471
Pseudo-Power	.984	1.413	1.747	2.031	2.282

FIGURE TN5.1B Percent of Variance Accounted for by Various Functions	
Function	**Percent of Variance Accounted for**
Power	92.5
Linear	94.2
Exponential	94.2
Logarithmic	86.1
Quadratic	95.6
Pseudo-Power	92.5

The reader should also note that the Pinnacle Plus software described in Chapter 6 uses the pseudo–power function because of the ease with which it can be embedded in preexisting software code.

Technical Note 5.2

The method of mounting evidence is based loosely on a Bayesian model of inference named for an English clergyman who did early work in probability and decision theory. The simplest version of Bayes's theorem states that for two events, A and B, the following relationship must hold: the probability of event A given event B is equal to the probability of the intersection of the events A and B (i.e., the probability of events A and B both occurring) divided by the probability of event B. In computational form, the Bayes's theorem translates to

$$p(A \mid B) = \frac{p(B \mid A)p(A)}{p(B \mid A)p(A) + p(B \mid \overline{A})p(\overline{A})}$$

where the symbol $\overline{A}$ means "not A" or the probability of event A not occurring.

Hays (1973) provides the following illustration. In the middle of the night, a man rises from his bed to take a sleeping pill. He goes to his bathroom and without turning on the light opens his medicine cabinet, grabs one of three bottles in the cabinet, and takes a pill from the bottle. When he returns to his bed, he starts to feel quite ill. Suddenly he recalls that two of the three bottles of pills in his medicine cabinet contain sleeping pills, but one contains a poison. He happens to have a medical text handy and looks up the symptoms associated with taking the poison. He finds that 80 percent of people in the general population exhibit the symptoms he is currently having when they take the poison, and 5 percent of people in the general population exhibit the symptoms he is having when they take a sleeping pill. If B represents the symptoms he is having, and A represents taking the poison, then

$$p(B \mid A) = .80$$

$$p(B \mid \overline{A}) = .05$$

If each bottle had equal probability of being chosen in the dark, then

$$p(A) = .33$$

$$p(\overline{A}) = .67$$

Substituting these quantities in the earlier formula gives

$$p(A \mid B) = \frac{(.80)(.33)}{(.80)(.33) + (.05)(.67)} = .89$$

Therefore, according to Bayes's theorem, the probability that the person has taken poison is .89.

Although the method of mounting evidence does not employ Bayes's theorem per se, it does employ the basic heuristic that what is known about a student's demonstrated level of performance for a given topic on previous assessments should inform a teacher's decision about a student's level of performance on a current assessment.

Technical Note 6.1

Willett (1988) has addressed the issue of the appropriate number of assessments in his discussion of measuring change in learning. Obviously, the more assessments (i.e., data points) the better, in terms of fitting a curve through the data. However, Willett exemplifies his approach to the measurement of knowledge change using four data points only (or four "waves" of data, to use his terminology).

It seems reasonable that teachers could fit in a minimum of four assessments for a given measurement topic within a grading period, especially when one considers the fact that a single test, quiz, and so on can be used to assess more than one topic. As mentioned in Chapter 6, I recommend five assessments for each topic. The issue to address is how accurately can a student's true score progression be estimated if only five data points are available? To answer this question, assume that a power function has been selected as the model of true score development.

Most discussions in the psychological literature of the power law as it relates to learning assume that the intervals between assessments are equal or nearly equal. This assumption would be difficult if not impossible to meet in the classroom. Teachers might not have the flexibility to give assessments in a set schedule (say, every other day). Also, the hiatus produced by weekends adds another mitigating factor.

There are at least two ways of addressing the issue of unequal intervals between assessments. These are depicted in Figure TN6.1. The first column in the figure represents 20 consecutive days during which students practice a given skill each day. The second column, True Score, is derived by applying the following power function: $y = 1.00x^{.45}$. In other words, the scores depicted in the second column are those that one can assume will be the true scores across 20 equally spaced practice sessions, given that learning follows the power function and a person begins with a score of 1.00.

Column 3 of Figure TN6.1 represents one way a teacher might keep track of student achievement, referred to as *order-based accounting*. Here, the teacher assigns five assessments over the 20-period interval and simply numbers the assessments consecutively without regard to differences in time intervals between them. It is easy to envision a classroom teacher doing this. That is, it is easy to imagine a teacher administering assessments when the curriculum allows, and then numbering these assessments consecutively without any regard for the intervals of time between assessments. The pertinent question relative to this

	FIGURE TN6.1				
	Order- and Time-Based Accounting				
Occasion	**True Score** $(y = 1.00x^{.45})$	**Order-Based Assessment #**	**Order-Based Prediction**	**Time-Based Assessment #**	**Time-Based Prediction**
1	1.000	1	1.104	1	1.000
2	1.366				
3	1.639				
4	1.866				
5	2.063				
6	2.239	2	1.977	6	2.239
7	2.400				
8	2.549				
9	2.688				
10	2.818				
11	2.940				
12	3.059	3	2.781	12	3.059
13	3.172				
14	3.279				
15	3.382				
16	3.482	4	3.542	16	3.482
17	3.579				
18	3.672				
19	3.762				
20	3.850	5	4.273	20	3.850

discussion is, how accurate is the estimate of a student's true score at the end of the 20-day period using this order-based accounting of assessments? To examine this issue, the true scores for these five assessments (Column 2) were regressed on the order-based assignment numbers (Column 3), and the predicted scores were computed using the power function. The predicted final score (i.e., predicted score for the 20th session) using this approach is 4.273, which is obviously an overestimate of the true final score of 3.850. In fact, this estimate exceeds the upper limit of the scale (i.e., the scale has no score higher than 4.0).

Column 5 of Figure TN6.1 depicts an alternate system of record keeping that might be referred to as a *time-based accounting* system. Here, the teacher assigns an identification number to each assessment that corresponds to the number of days students have had to practice or review a given trait. Thus, the second assessment that is given to students (in terms of its order) is given an assessment number of 6 because it occurs 6 days into the instruction/assessment cycle, the third assessment (in order) is given an assessment number of 12 because it occurs 12 days into the instruction/assessment cycle, and so on. In this system, then, assessment numbers mirror the actual point in time in the instruction/assessment cycle. When the true scores for these five assessments are regressed on the time-based assessment number, the predicted final scores perfectly match the true scores.

This simulation is contrived but makes an important point. Specifically, the time-based system provides for a more precise estimation of a given student's true score than the order-based system of accounting. In fact, the implication is that the time-based system provides for a very accurate estimate of the final true score even when only one-fourth of the data points (i.e., 5 of 20 situations) are used.

Technical Note 6.2

The last decade has seen great interest in the theory base for classroom assessment. In fact, in 2003 an entire issue of *Educational Measurement: Issues and Practice* (Volume 22, Number 4) was devoted to a discussion of the current status of classroom assessment theory. Virtually every measurement expert who contributed to that issue either explicitly or implicitly noted that both classical test theory (CTT) and item response theory (IRT) were designed for large-scale assessments and do not transfer well to classroom assessment. Virtually every article in that volume proposed a new theory for or new approaches to estimating the reliability (or other psychometric properties) of individual classroom assessments. Missing from the discussion was a consideration of the psychometric properties of aggregate or summary scores of student achievement. The discussions in Chapters 3, 4, 5, and 6 indicate that use of formative classroom assessment forces consideration of psychometric properties (particularly reliability) beyond the single assessment. The need to consider many forms of reliability has also been acknowledged by Frisbie (2005). Specifically, when the assumption is made that the true score changes over assessments (as is the necessary case with formative assessments), reliability can be approached from two perspectives.

The first perspective is the reliability of scores from a particular assessment. This is typically addressed by computing some sort of reliability coefficient or generalizability coefficient based on one or more studies that is then assumed to represent the reliability of that particular assessment, although Frisbie (2005) has commented on the inaccuracy of such an interpretation. (See Technical Note 3.4 for a discussion.) Regarding the measurement scale presented in Chapter 3, such studies have been conducted (see Marzano, 2002a).

The second perspective is that of the reliability of sets of scores for each subject—more specifically, the reliability of the mathematical model used to describe the change in scores from testing occasion to testing occasion. Willett (1988) has documented the rich history of this literature, but to date, it has not been applied to classroom assessment. As described by Willett (1985), the basic measurement model for this endeavor is

$$X_{ip} = F_p(t_i) + e_{ip} \tag{1}$$

where the subscript i denotes the occasion of measurement, t_i is the time at which the ith occasion of measurement occurred, and the subscript p indicates the person being measured. The symbol F_p represents true status for person p, and the parenthetical inclusion of the time at which the ith measurement occurred indicates that F_p is changing (growing) over time. Consequently, the notation $F_p(t_i)$ represents a function describing the true status of individual p at varying times; e_{ip} represents the measurement error associated with person p at time i.

Contrast this formative measurement model with the summative model from classical test theory:

$$X_p = F_p + e_p \tag{2}$$

Here F_p is the true status of person p. The absence of the parenthetical expression (t_i) illustrates that the classical measurement model assumes a fixed true status. From Equation 1, one might infer that a critical aspect of constructing a viable formative measurement model is to identify the most appropriate growth function, $F_p(t_i)$. Here, two growth functions are considered: the difference score function and the multiwave linear function.

The Difference Score Function

The simplest growth function that might be used as the basis for classroom assessment is the difference between initial and final status. In such a situation, a classroom teacher would use an initial test of student achievement on the content to be covered in a unit of instruction. Each student's score on this initial assessment would be subtracted from the student's score on an end-of-unit test under the assumption that initial and final tests are parallel. The research on the sensitization effects of a pretest indicates that classroom teachers might even use the same test for both occasions (Wilson & Putnam, 1982). The mathematical model for this growth function is

$$D_p = X_{fp} - X_{1p} \tag{3}$$

where X_{fp} is the final measurement for person p (e.g., the final assessment during a unit of instruction) and X_{1p} is the first measurement for person p. There is a simple relationship between the observed difference score and the underlying change in true score that has occurred between t_f and t_1:

$$D_p = \Delta_p + e_p^* \tag{4}$$

where $\Delta_p = F_p(t_f) - F_p(t_1)$ and $e_p^* = e_{fp} - e_{ip}$. As a consequence of the assumption of independence of error terms, one can conclude the e^* is normally distributed with zero mean and variance $2\sigma_e$. Additionally, it can be shown that the observed difference score for individual p is an unbiased estimate of the quantity Δ_p. Rogosa, Brandt, and Zimowsky (1982) emphasize the fact that the observed difference score is an unbiased estimate of the true difference score regardless of the magnitude of the measurement error. This is necessarily so because the expected value of the observed difference score for person p is the true difference score for person p. Willett (1988) notes that in spite of "this obvious and optimal statistical property" the difference score has been criticized "so thoroughly and continuously over the years that investigators have become wary of its use" (p. 366), most notably for its perceived low reliability. Although it is true that difference scores will frequently exhibit low reliability, this does not necessarily mean they exhibit poor precision at the level of individual difference scores. An examination of the conceptual underpinnings of the reliability of difference scores provides some insight into the issue.

The population reliability of difference scores $p(D)$ is defined as the ratio of variance of Δ_p to variance of D_p over all individuals in the population. Given that $p(D)$ is expressed in terms of observed differences, Willett (1988, p. 368) offers the following formula, which requires no simplifying assumptions:

$$p(D) = \frac{\sigma_{x1}^2 p(x_1 x_1) + \sigma_{xf}^2 p(x_f x_f) - 2\sigma_{x1}\sigma_{xf} p(x_1 x_f)}{(\sigma_{x1}^2) + (\sigma_{xf}^2) - 2\sigma_{x1}\sigma_{xf}(px_1 x_f)} \tag{5}$$

Here $p(x_1x_1)$ and $p(x_fx_f)$ are the population reliabilities for x_1 and x_f, $p(x_1x_f)$ is the population correlation between initial scores (x_1) and final status scores (x_f). The fact that the term containing the correlation between initial and final status is subtracted in both the numerator and denominator is the reason commonly given for assumed poor reliability of difference scores. As Willett (1988) explains:

> Because the variances in the first two terms of the numerator are multiplied by their respective reliabilities and are, therefore, smaller than the equivalent terms in the denominator, the subtraction of the term containing the between-wave correlation in both the numerator and the denominator ensures that when $p(x_1x_f)$ is large and positive, then $p(D)$ will be low. And, as the correlation of initial and final status is frequently misinterpreted as an index of construct validity, authors are apt to report that the difference score cannot be both reliable and valid simultaneously. (pp. 368–369)

To illustrate the impact of a high correlation between initial and final status on the reliability of difference scores, consider the situation in which $p(x_1x_f)$ is zero. The term subtracted in the numerator and denominator becomes zero, rendering Equation 5 to be

$$p(D) = \frac{\sigma_{x1}^2 p(x_1x_1) + \sigma_{xf}^2 p(x_fx_f)}{\sigma_{x1}^2 + \sigma_{xf}^2}$$

(6)

In Equation 6, the reliability of the difference scores reduces to the variance-weighted average of $p(x_1x_1)$ and $p(x_fx_f)$. If we assume that $\sigma^2(x_1) = 4$, $\sigma^2(x_f) = 9$, $p(x_1x_1) = .90$, and $p(x_fx_f) = .80$, then, $p(D) = .83$. However, if we assume a moderate correlation between initial and final status of .50, then $p(D)$ is reduced to .69 (using Equation 5).

Given that the correlation between tests of initial and final status is usually quite high, the practical implication is that the computed reliability of difference scores will almost always be low. As Feldt and Brennan (1989) note:

> When one looks at the reported data for standardized achievement tests, as in reading, it is not uncommon to find reliabilities of status scores in grades 5 and 6 of about .88 and year-to-year correlations of .82. Thus growth measures often have reliabilities in the neighborhood of .33 or lower. Yet, no one would deny that the typical fifth-grade student makes considerable progress in a year's time. (p. 119)

Willett (1988, p. 369) provides further insight into the reliability of difference scores using the perspective of the homogeneity (or lack thereof) of individual growth rates. He notes that a more illustrative formulation of the reliability of difference scores is

$$p(D) = \frac{\sigma_\Delta^2}{\sigma_\Delta^2 + 2\sigma_e^2}$$

(7)

Here it is clear that the reliability of the difference score increases as the differences in true change increase among individuals. As Willett (1988) notes,

> Thus, the greater the individual differences in true growth, the greater the reliability of the difference score. Where there are no individual differences in true growth to detect (i.e., when σ_Δ^2 is equal to zero and all the individual true score growth trajectories are parallel), the reliability of the difference score can only be zero, regardless of the precision with which measurement has been carried out. (p. 370)

Ultimately, an analysis of the theoretical underpinnings of the reliability of difference scores leads one to the conclusion that this construct is not well suited to the task of examining the viability of individual difference scores. By definition, "Reliability is a measure of inter-individual differentiations and can only be defined over a group or population" (Rogosa et al., 1982, p. 730). Given that heterogeneity of growth rates is a prerequisite for high reliability of difference scores, assessment situations in which growth rates are homogeneous will produce low reliabilities but tell one little about the precision of measurement. As Rogosa and colleagues note, "Although individual differences in growth are necessary for high reliability, the absence of such differences does not preclude meaningful assessment of individual change" (p. 731).

In summary, despite the characteristically low reliabilities associated with them, initial to final status difference scores are a viable candidate for the growth function in a formative measurement model. Specifically, teachers might administer a comprehensive assessment at the beginning and end of a unit and use the difference scores as viable estimates of student academic growth. This said, a multipoint or multiwave approach has a number of advantages over a difference score approach.

The Multiwave Linear Function

Although this discussion supports the use of difference scores as estimates of students' learning, the practice is still problematic. Even though estimates of the reliability of difference scores are not well suited to the assessment of individual change, they should still be estimated. However, such estimates require information not easily obtained by the classroom teacher. As Willett (1988) notes,

> In addition to the sample variances and correlation provided by the two waves of growth data, the investigator must also have two supplementary pieces of information: the estimated reliability of observed status on each of the two occasions of measurement. Either this supplementary information must be obtained externally to the growth investigations (i.e., from a test manual or a previous empirical reliability study), or duplicate measurements of observed status must be made on each subject at each of the two time points to permit in situ estimation of required reliability. (p. 371)

Obviously, these requirements for supplemental information do not fit well in the context of classroom assessments. An approach that more readily allows for the estimation of a reliability index that is more meaningful to the estimation of individual growth is the use of multipoint or multiwave data. Additionally, multiwave data provide for a better estimate of true growth than do difference scores:

> Taking a snapshot of individual status on each of two occasions does not permit the investigator to visualize the intricacies of the underlying individual growth with any great certainty. . . . Indeed, to measure individual growth adequately, more information on that growth in the form of multi-wave data is required. When multi-wave data are available on each of the subjects in the sample, the investigator can examine detailed empirical growth—trajectory plots that summarize the observed growth of each individual over time. (Willett, 1988, pp. 384–385)

In a classroom situation, multiwave data might be collected by a teacher administering multiple assessments designed and scored in the fashion described in Chapters 3 and 4.

One way to conceptualize the advantages of multiwave data is to think of the difference score as an estimate of the regression weight for the linear function representing an individual's growth when only two data points are available. Indeed, when only two data points are available, the regression weight for the straight-line function for an individual student is

$$\frac{x_f - x_1}{t_f - t_1}$$

(8)

This is directly proportioned to the raw difference score (see Willett, 1988, p. 385; Rogosa et al., 1982, p. 728).

Modeling growth using multiwave data is based on the assumption that learning over time follows a definable mathematical function and that observed measurements over time are imprecise estimates of the growth function.

> When an individual is growing, it is as though the underlying true growth is continuing smoothly and unobserved over time, but periodically, the investigator observes the growth with some fallible measuring instrument. In this way, the individual's observed growth record is assembled and it consists of a chronological series of discrete measurements, each of which is an unknown combination of true status and measurement error. What is of fundamental interest to the investigator, of course, is the underlying, continuous true growth trajectory; the multiple entries in the observed growth record are simply a fallible lens through which the true individual growth is viewed. (Willett, 1988, pp. 386–387)

R. Mead and D. J. Pike (1975) list a variety of algebraic functions that might be used to model the true growth function for individuals, as do Rogosa and colleagues

(1982). Many of these are discussed in Technical Note 5.1. For this discussion, the linear or straight-line function is used, although the logic articulated here applies to the other functions (Seigel, 1975). Specifically, when the pseudo-power function is used as a viable estimate of the power function, the logic for the straight-line function discussed here applies to the natural log transformations.

In the context of the present discussion, the straight-line function modeling these data would be represented as

$$F_p(t) = F_p(t^*) + B_p(t - t^*) \tag{9}$$

where $F_p(t^*)$ represents true initial status, $(t - t^*)$ represents the time differential between occasion of measurement t and occasion t^*, and B is the regression coefficient that represents the (constant) rate of change from occasion to occasion (see Willett, 1988, p. 390).

Given the use of the linear function, the basic measurement model now becomes

$$X_{ip} = F_p(t^*) + B_p(t - t^*) + e_{ip} \tag{10}$$

For the purposes of estimating individual growth, the key parameter is B_p—the coefficient for the regression of the observed score on the change in occasion of measurement, or the rate of change in the observed score for one unit of change in occasion of measurement (assuming equal distances between units). The precision of this estimate is analogous to the precision of estimate of an individual's true status at a given point in time.

The multiple data points allow for estimations of precision and reliability. Willett (1988, p. 402) explains that the relationship between the population variance of growth rates (σ_B^2) and the sample variance ($\sigma_{\hat{B}}^2$) is

$$\sigma_{\hat{B}}^2 = \sigma_B^2 + \frac{\sigma_e^2}{SST} \tag{11}$$

where SST is the sum of squares for the observation times—the squared deviations of the observation times about their mean ($\Sigma[ti - \overline{t}]$). This is a measure of the spread of occasion of measurement. The variance due to measurement error is represented by σ_e^2. Equation 11 illustrates that the sample variance of the growth rates will overestimate the true variance of the growth rates.

Given that multiwave data are available, measurement error variance for each person can be computed and, consequently, used in the estimate of the population variance of growth rates. Specifically, given that the growth model fitted to the data is a correct one, the differences between the observed scores and predicted scores estimate the measurement error (*MSE*) on each occasion of measurement. As Willett (1988) notes,

> The magnitude of the measurement error can be found directly from these residuals. Under the assumptions of this paper, an estimate of σ_e^2 can be found quite simply by summing the squared residuals . . . [across] occasions and persons, and then dividing by the total degrees of freedom. (p. 403)

By algebraic manipulation, the sum of the squared residuals can be shown to be equal to the simple average of the *MSE* for each person. Therefore,

$$\hat{\sigma}_e^{\,2} = \frac{\sum\limits_{p=1}^{n} MSE_p}{n}$$

(12)

Estimating the Reliability of Growth Rates

From a semantic perspective, the reliability of growth rates is defined as the ratio of variance of the true growth rates over the variance of the observed growth rates. Because the variance of the observed growth rates can be computed as well as a viable estimate of the variance of the true growth rates, the population reliability of the growth rates can be estimated via the following formula:

$$p(\hat{B}) = \frac{\sigma_B^2}{\sigma_B^2 + \dfrac{\sigma_e^2}{SST}}$$

(13)

Thus, in a population that has plenty of criss-crossing of true growth trajectories, considerable reliability is possible in practice. On the other hand, if there are no interindividual differences in the rate of true growth ($\sigma_B^2 = 0$), then all of the true growth trajectories will be parallel and the growth reliability can only be zero, regardless of the precision with which measurement has been achieved (Willett, 1988, p. 404).

In summary, the use of formative assessments obtained over time in the classroom allows not only for estimation of individual students' true scores at the end of a learning period but also for the estimation of individual growth trajectories, estimation of measurement error for individual students, and estimation of the reliabilities of the growth trajectory for the class considered as a group.

Finally, Rogosa and colleagues (1982) provide a number of "mottos" for the measurement of individual change that apply nicely to the present discussion regarding classroom assessment:

○ Two waves of data are better than one but maybe not much better. Two data points provide meager information on individual change, and, thus, the measurement of change often will require more than the traditional pre-post data.

○ When only two waves of data are available, the difference score is a natural and useful estimate of individual change.

○ There is more than one way to judge a measure of change. Reliability is not the "be all and end all" in the measurement of change. Statistical properties are important.

○ Low reliability does not necessarily mean lack of precision.

○ The difference between two fallible measures can be nearly as reliable as the measures themselves. (p. 744)

Using the well-articulated theory of measurement of change, these mottos can be executed to form the basis of a formative model of classroom assessment.

Appendix A: Half-Point Scores Contrasted with Whole-Point Scores

One way to fully understand the complete scoring scale is to contrast the half-point scores with the whole-point scores that bound them, as shown in this table.

Half-Point Score	Descriptions of Half-Point Scores and Related Whole-Point Scores
0.5	A score of 0.0 indicates that . . . • *with help* the student demonstrates no understanding of the more complex ideas and processes (Type II) or the simpler details and processes (Type I). A score of 1.0 indicates that . . . • *with help* the student demonstrates a partial understanding of the more complex ideas and processes (Type II) as well as some of the simpler details and processes (Type I). A score of 0.5 indicates that . . . • *with help* the student demonstrates a partial understanding of some of the simpler details and processes (Type I) but not of the more complex ideas and processes (Type II).
1.5	A score of 1.0 indicates that . . . • *with help* the student demonstrates a partial understanding of the more complex ideas and processes (Type II) as well as some of the simpler details and processes (Type I). A score of 2.0 indicates that . . . • the student demonstrates errors or omissions with the more complex ideas and processes (Type II) but not with the simpler details and processes (Type I). A score of 1.5 indicates that . . . • the student demonstrates major errors and omissions with the more complex ideas and processes (Type II) but exhibits *partial* knowledge of the simpler details and processes, although there are still errors (Type I).
2.5	A score of 2.0 indicates that . . . • the student demonstrates errors or omissions with the more complex ideas and processes (Type II) but not with the simpler details and processes (Type I). A score of 3.0 indicates . . . • the student demonstrates no errors or omissions relative to the more complex ideas and processes (Type II) or the simpler details and processes (Type I). A score of 2.5 indicates that . . . • the student demonstrates no errors or omissions with the simpler details and processes (Type I) and exhibits *partial* knowledge of more complex ideas and processes (Type II).
3.5	A score of 3.0 indicates that . . . • the student demonstrates no errors or omissions relative to the more complex ideas and processes (Type II) or the simpler details and processes (Type I). A score of 4.0 indicates that . . . • the student demonstrates inferences and applications that go beyond what was taught in class (Type III). A score of 3.5 indicates that . . . • the student demonstrates partial success at the inferences and applications that go beyond what was taught in class.

Appendix B: Score Descriptions
for a Sample Measurement Topic from Language Arts

	Subject Area: Language Arts
	Measurement Topic: Reading for Main Idea
	Grades 9–10 (Lower Division)
Score 4.0	In addition to Score 3.0 performance, the student goes beyond what was taught by . . . • explaining which parts of a pattern are explicit and which parts must be inferred, and • explaining and defending inferences regarding patterns.
	Score 3.5 In addition to Score 3.0 performance, partial success at inferences and applications that go beyond what was taught.
Score 3.0	While reading grade-appropriate material, the student identifies the major patterns in the text, such as . . . • complex causal relationships that are explicit and implied, • arguments with complex systems of support that are explicit and implied, • problems with complex solutions that are explicit and implied, and • complex plots with multiple story lines that are explicit and implied. The student exhibits no major errors or omissions.
	Score 2.5 No major errors or omissions regarding the simpler details and processes and partial knowledge of the more complex ideas and processes.
Score 2.0	The student exhibits no major errors or omissions regarding the simpler details, such as identifying . . . • complex causal relationships that are explicit, • arguments with complex systems of support that are explicit, • problems with complex solutions that are explicit, and • complex plots with multiple story lines that are explicit. However, the student exhibits major errors or omissions on the more complex ideas and processes.
	Score 1.5 Partial knowledge of the simpler details and processes but major errors or omissions regarding the more complex ideas and processes.
Score 1.0	With help, the student demonstrates a partial understanding of some of the simpler details and processes and some of the more complex ideas and processes.
	Score 0.5 With help, a partial understanding of some of the simpler details and processes but not the more complex ideas and processes.
Score 0.0	Even with help, the student demonstrates no understanding or skill.

	Subject Area: Language Arts	
	Measurement Topic: Reading for Main Idea	
	Grade 8	
Score 4.0	In addition to Score 3.0 performance, the student goes beyond what was taught by . . . • explaining which parts of a pattern are explicit and which parts must be inferred, • explaining and defending inferences regarding patterns.	
	Score 3.5	In addition to Score 3.0 performance, partial success at inferences and applications that go beyond what was taught.
Score 3.0	While reading grade-appropriate material, the student identifies and articulates the major patterns in the text, such as . . . • complex causal relationships that are explicit and implied, • basic arguments that are explicit and implied, • problems with complex solutions that are explicit and implied, • complex plots with multiple story lines that are explicit and implied. The student exhibits no major errors or omissions.	
	Score 2.5	No major errors or omissions regarding the simpler details and processes and partial knowledge of the more complex ideas and processes.
Score 2.0	The student exhibits no major errors or omissions regarding the simpler details, such as identifying . . . • complex causal relationships that are explicit, • basic arguments that are explicit, • problems with complex solutions that are explicit, • complex plots with multiple story lines that are explicit. However, the student exhibits major errors or omissions on the more complex ideas and processes.	
	Score 1.5	Partial knowledge of the simpler details and processes but major errors or omissions regarding the more complex ideas and processes.
Score 1.0	With help, the student demonstrates a partial understanding of some of the simpler details and processes and some of the more complex ideas and processes.	
	Score 0.5	With help, a partial understanding of some of the simpler details and processes but not the more complex ideas and processes.
Score 0.0	Even with help, the student demonstrates no understanding or skill.	

	Subject Area: Language Arts
	Measurement Topic: Reading for Main Idea
	Grade 7

Score 4.0	**In addition to Score 3.0 performance, the student goes beyond what was taught by ...**
	   • **explaining which parts of a pattern are explicit and which parts must be inferred, and**
	   • **explaining and defending inferences regarding patterns.**	

	Score 3.5	In addition to Score 3.0 performance, partial success at inferences and applications that go beyond what was taught.

Score 3.0	**While reading grade-appropriate material, the student identifies and articulates the major patterns in the text, such as ...**
	   • **complex causal relationships that are explicit and implied,**
	   • **basic arguments that are explicit and implied,**
	   • **problems with complex solutions that are explicit and implied, and**
	   • **plots with single story lines that are explicit and implied.**
	The student exhibits no major errors or omissions.	

	Score 2.5	No major errors or omissions regarding the simpler details and processes and partial knowledge of the more complex ideas and processes.

Score 2.0	**No major errors or omissions regarding the simpler details, such as identifying ...**
	   • **complex causal relationships that are explicit,**
	   • **basic arguments that are explicit,**
	   • **problems with complex solutions that are explicit, and**
	   • **plots with single story lines that are explicit.**
	However, the student exhibits major errors or omissions on the more complex ideas and processes.	

	Score 1.5	Partial knowledge of the simpler details and processes but major errors or omissions regarding the more complex ideas and processes.
Score 1.0	**With help, the student demonstrates a partial understanding of some of the simpler details and processes and some of the more complex ideas and processes.**	
	Score 0.5	With help, a partial understanding of some of the simpler details and processes but not the more complex ideas and processes.
Score 0.0	**Even with help, the student demonstrates no understanding or skill.**	

	Subject Area: Language Arts
	Measurement Topic: Reading for Main Idea
	Grade 6

Score 4.0	In addition to Score 3.0 performance, the student goes beyond what was taught by . . . • explaining which parts of a pattern are explicit and which parts must be inferred, and • explaining and defending inferences regarding patterns.	
	Score 3.5	In addition to Score 3.0 performance, partial success at inferences and applications that go beyond what was taught.
Score 3.0	While reading grade-appropriate material, the student identifies and articulates the major patterns in the text, such as . . . • complex causal relationships that are explicit and implied, • basic arguments that are explicit and implied, • complex chronologies that are explicit and implied, • problems with basic solutions that are explicit and implied, and • plots with single story lines that are explicit and implied. The student exhibits no major errors or omissions.	
	Score 2.5	No major errors or omissions regarding the simpler details and processes and partial knowledge of the more complex ideas and processes.
Score 2.0	The student exhibits no major errors or omissions regarding the simpler details, such as identifying . . . • complex causal relationships that are explicit, • basic arguments that are explicit, • complex chronologies that are explicit, • problems with basic solutions that are explicit, and • plots with single story lines that are explicit. However, the student exhibits major errors or omissions on the more complex ideas and processes.	
	Score 1.5	Partial knowledge of the simpler details and processes but major errors or omissions regarding the more complex ideas and processes.
Score 1.0	With help, the student demonstrates a partial understanding of some of the simpler details and processes and some of the more complex ideas and processes.	
	Score 0.5	With help, a partial understanding of some of the simpler details and processes but not the more complex ideas and processes.
Score 0.0	Even with help, the student demonstrates no understanding or skill.	

	Subject Area: Language Arts
	Measurement Topic: Reading for Main Idea
	Grade 5
Score 4.0	In addition to Score 3.0 performance, the student goes beyond what was taught by . . . • explaining which parts of a pattern are explicit and which parts must be inferred, and • explaining and defending inferences regarding patterns.
	Score 3.5 — In addition to Score 3.0 performance, partial success at inferences and applications that go beyond what was taught.
Score 3.0	While reading grade-appropriate material, the student identifies and articulates the major patterns in the text, such as . . . • complex causal relationships that are explicit and implied, • complex chronologies that are explicit and implied, • problems with basic solutions that are explicit and implied, and • plots with single story lines that are explicit and implied. The student exhibits no major errors or omissions.
	Score 2.5 — No major errors or omissions regarding the simpler details and processes and partial knowledge of the more complex ideas and processes.
Score 2.0	The student exhibits no major errors or omissions regarding the simpler details, such as identifying . . . • complex causal relationships that are explicit, • complex chronologies that are explicit, • problems with basic solutions that are explicit, and • plots with single story lines that are explicit. However, the student exhibits major errors or omissions on the more complex ideas and processes.
	Score 1.5 — Partial knowledge of the simpler details and processes but major errors or omissions regarding the more complex ideas and processes.
Score 1.0	With help, the student demonstrates a partial understanding of some of the simpler details and processes and some of the more complex ideas and processes.
	Score 0.5 — With help, a partial understanding of some of the simpler details and processes but not the more complex ideas and processes.
Score 0.0	Even with help, the student demonstrates no understanding or skill.

	Subject Area: Language Arts	
	Measurement Topic: Reading for Main Idea	
	Grade 4	
Score 4.0	**In addition to Score 3.0 performance, the student goes beyond what was taught by . . .** • **explaining which parts of a pattern are explicit and which parts must be inferred, and** • **explaining and defending inferences regarding patterns.**	
	Score 3.5	In addition to Score 3.0 performance, partial success at inferences and applications that go beyond what was taught.
Score 3.0	**While reading grade-appropriate material, the student identifies and articulates the major patterns in the text, such as . . .** • **basic cause and effect that is explicit and implied,** • **simple chronologies that are explicit and implied,** • **problems with basic solutions that are explicit and implied, and** • **plots with single story lines that are explicit and implied.** **The student exhibits no major errors or omissions.**	
	Score 2.5	No major errors or omissions regarding the simpler details and processes and partial knowledge of the more complex ideas and processes.
Score 2.0	**The student exhibits no major errors or omissions regarding the simpler details, such as identifying . . .** • **basic cause and effect that is explicit,** • **simple chronologies that are explicit,** • **problems with basic solutions that are explicit, and** • **plots with single story lines that are explicit.** **However, the student exhibits major errors or omissions on the more complex ideas and processes.**	
	Score 1.5	Partial knowledge of the simpler details and processes but major errors or omissions regarding the more complex ideas and processes.
Score 1.0	**With help, the student demonstrates a partial understanding of some of the simpler details and processes and some of the more complex ideas and processes.**	
	Score 0.5	With help, a partial understanding of some of the simpler details and processes but not the more complex ideas and processes.
Score 0.0	**Even with help, the student demonstrates no understanding or skill.**	

	Subject Area: Language Arts
	Measurement Topic: Reading for Main Idea
	Grade 3
Score 4.0	**In addition to Score 3.0 performance, the student goes beyond what was taught by ...** • **explaining which parts of a pattern are explicit and which parts must be inferred, and** • **explaining and defending inferences regarding patterns.**
	Score 3.5 In addition to Score 3.0 performance, partial success at inferences and applications that go beyond what was taught.
Score 3.0	**While reading grade-appropriate material, the student identifies and articulates the major patterns in the text, such as ...** • **basic cause and effect that is explicit and implied,** • **simple chronologies that are explicit and implied,** • **problems with basic solutions that are explicit and implied, and** • **plots with single story lines that are explicit and implied.** **The student exhibits no major errors or omissions.**
	Score 2.5 No major errors or omissions regarding the simpler details and processes and partial knowledge of the more complex ideas and processes.
Score 2.0	**The student exhibits no major errors or omissions regarding the simpler details, such as identifying ...** • **basic cause and effect that is explicit,** • **simple chronologies that are explicit,** • **problems with basic solutions that are explicit, and** • **plots with single story lines that are explicit.** **However, the student exhibits major errors or omissions on the more complex ideas and processes.**
	Score 1.5 Partial knowledge of the simpler details and processes but major errors or omissions regarding the more complex ideas and processes.
Score 1.0	**With help, the student demonstrates a partial understanding of some of the simpler details and processes and some of the more complex ideas and processes.**
	Score 0.5 With help, a partial understanding of some of the simpler details and processes but not the more complex ideas and processes.
Score 0.0	**Even with help, the student demonstrates no understanding or skill.**

	Subject Area: Language Arts	
	Measurement Topic: Reading for Main Idea	
	Grade 2	
Score 4.0	In addition to Score 3.0 performance, the student goes beyond what was taught by . . . • explaining which parts of a pattern are explicit and which parts must be inferred, and • explaining and defending inferences regarding patterns.	
	Score 3.5	In addition to Score 3.0 performance, partial success at inferences and applications that go beyond what was taught.
Score 3.0	While reading grade-appropriate material, the student identifies and articulates the major patterns in the text, such as . . . • basic cause and effect that is explicit and implied, and • plots with single story lines that are explicit and implied. The student exhibits no major errors or omissions.	
	Score 2.5	No major errors or omissions regarding the simpler details and processes and partial knowledge of the more complex ideas and processes.
Score 2.0	The student exhibits no major errors or omissions regarding the simpler details, such as identifying . . . • basic cause and effect that is explicit, and • plots with single story lines that are explicit. However, the student exhibits major errors or omissions on the more complex ideas and processes.	
	Score 1.5	Partial knowledge of the simpler details and processes but major errors or omissions regarding the more complex ideas and processes.
Score 1.0	With help, the student demonstrates a partial understanding of some of the simpler details and processes and some of the more complex ideas and processes.	
	Score 0.5	With help, a partial understanding of some of the simpler details and processes but not the more complex ideas and processes.
Score 0.0	Even with help, the student demonstrates no understanding or skill.	

	Subject Area: Language Arts	
	Measurement Topic: Reading for Main Idea	
	Grade 1	

Score 4.0	**In addition to Score 3.0 performance, the student goes beyond what was taught by . . .**
	   • **explaining which parts of a pattern are explicit and which parts must be inferred, and**
	   • **explaining and defending inferences regarding patterns.**	

	Score 3.5	In addition to Score 3.0 performance, partial success at inferences and applications that go beyond what was taught.
Score 3.0	**While reading grade-appropriate material, the student identifies and articulates the major patterns in the text, such as . . .** • **plots with simple story lines that are explicit and implied.** **The student exhibits no major errors or omissions.**	
	Score 2.5	No major errors or omissions regarding the simpler details and processes and partial knowledge of the more complex ideas and processes.
Score 2.0	**The student exhibits no major errors or omissions regarding the simpler details, such as identifying . . .** • **plots with simple story lines that are explicit.** **However, the student exhibits major errors or omissions on the more complex ideas and processes.**	
	Score 1.5	Partial knowledge of the simpler details and processes but major errors or omissions regarding the more complex ideas and processes.
Score 1.0	**With help, the student demonstrates a partial understanding of some of the simpler details and processes and some of the more complex ideas and processes.**	
	Score 0.5	With help, a partial understanding of some of the simpler details and processes but not the more complex ideas and processes.
Score 0.0	**Even with help, the student demonstrates no understanding or skill.**	

REFERENCES

Ainsworth, L. (2003a). *Power standards: Identifying the standards that matter most.* Denver, CO: Advance Learning Press.

Ainsworth, L. (2003b). *Unwrapping the standards: A simple process to make standards manageable.* Denver, CO: Advance Learning Press.

Ainsworth, L., & Viegut, D. (2006). *Common formative assessments.* Thousand Oaks, CA: Corwin Press.

Airasian, P. W. (1994). *Classroom assessment* (2nd ed.). New York: McGraw-Hill.

American Association for the Advancement of Science. (2001). *Atlas of science literacy.* Washington, DC: American Association for the Advancement of Science and the National Science Teachers Association.

Anderson, J. R. (1983). *The architecture of cognition.* Cambridge, MA: Harvard University Press.

Anderson, J. R. (1995). *Learning and memory: An integrated approach.* New York: Wiley.

Anderson, J. R., Greeno, J. G., Reder, L. M., & Simon, H. A. (2000). Perspectives on learning, thinking and activity. *Educational Researcher, 29*(4), 11–13.

Anderson, J. R., Reder, L. M., & Simon, H. A. (1995). *Applications and misapplications of cognitive psychology to mathematics education.* Unpublished paper, Carnegie Mellon University, Department of Psychology, Pittsburgh, PA. Available: http://act.psy.cmu.edu/personal/ja/misapplied.html

Anderson, J. R., Reder, L. M., & Simon, H. A. (1996). Situated learning and education. *Educational Researcher, 25*(4), 5–11.

Andrade, H. G., & Boulay, B. A. (2003). Role of rubric-referenced self-assessment in learning to write. *Journal of Educational Research, 97*(1), 21–34.

Atkinson, J. W. (1957). Motivational determinants of risk taking behavior. *Psychological Review, 64,* 359–372.

Atkinson, J. W. (1964). *An introduction to motivation.* Princeton, NJ: Van Nostrand.

Atkinson, J. W. (1987). Michigan studies of fear of failure. In F. Halisch & J. Kuhl (Eds.), *Motivation, intention, and volition* (pp. 47–60). Berlin: Springer.

Atkinson, J. W., & Raynor, J. O. (1974). *Motivation and achievement.* New York: Wiley.

Baker, E. L., Aschbacher, P. R., Niemi, D., & Sato, E. (1992). CRESST performance assessment models: Assessing content area explanations. Los Angeles: National Center for Research on Evaluation, Standards, and Student Testing, University of California.

Bangert-Drowns, R. L., Kulik, C. C., Kulik, J. A., & Morgan, M. T. (1991). The instructional effect of feedback on test-like events. *Review of Educational Research, 61*(2), 213–238.

Bangert-Drowns, R. L., Kulik, J. A., & Kulik, C. C. (1991). Effects of classroom testing. *Journal of Educational Research, 85*(2), 89–99.

Birnbaum, A. (1957). *Efficient design and use of tests of mental ability for various decision-making problems.* Series Report No. 58-16. Project No. 7755-23, USAF School of Aviation Medicine. Randolph Air Force Base, TX.

Birnbaum, A. (1958a). *Further considerations of efficiency in tests of mental ability.* Series Report No. 17. Project No. 7755-23, USAF School of Aviation Medicine. Randolph Air Force Base, TX.

Birnbaum, A. (1958b). *On the estimation of mental ability.* Series Report No. 15. Project No. 7755-23, USAF School of Aviation Medicine. Randolph Air Force Base, TX.

Black, P., & Wiliam, D. (1998). Assessment and classroom learning. *Assessment in Education, 5*(1), 7–75.

Bloom, B. S. (1968). Learning for mastery. *Evaluation Comment, 1*(2), 1–12.

Bloom, B. S. (1976). *Human characteristics and school learning.* New York: McGraw-Hill.

Bloom, B. S. (1984). The search for methods of group instruction as effective as one-to-one tutoring. *Educational Leadership, 42*(3), 4–17.

Bock, R. D. (1997). A brief history of item response theory. *Educational Measurement, Issue and Practice, 16*(4), 21–33.

Boyer, E. L. (1983). *High school: A report on secondary education in America.* New York: Harper & Row.

Boyer, E. L. (1995). *The basic school: A community for learning.* Princeton, NJ: Carnegie Foundation for the Advancement of Teaching.

Brookhart, S. M. (1994). Teachers' grading: Practices and theory. *Applied Measurement in Education, 7*(4), 279–301.

Brookhart, S. M. (2004). *Grading.* Columbus, OH: Pearson.

Burt, C. (1957). The distribution of intelligence. *British Journal of Psychology, 48,* 161–175.

Butler, D. L., & Winne, P. H. (1995). Feedback and self-regulated learning: A theoretical synthesis. *Review of Educational Research, 65*(3), 245–281.

Cahen, S., & Davis, D. (1987). A between-grade levels approach to the investigation of the absolute effects of schooling on achievement. *American Educational Research Journal, 24,* 1–2.

Carnevale, A. P., Gainer, L. J., & Meltzer, A. S. (1990). *Workplace basics: The essential skills employers want.* San Francisco: Jossey-Bass.

Carroll, J. B. (1963). A model of school learning. *Teachers College Record, 64,* 723–733.

Carroll, J. B. (1989). The Carroll model: A 25-year retrospective and prospective view. *Educational Researcher, 8*(1), 26–31.

Cohen, J. C., Cohen, P., West, S. G., & Aiken, L. S. (2003). *Applied multiple regression/correlation analysis for the behavioral sciences* (3rd ed.). Mahwah, NJ: Erlbaum.

Coladarci, T., Smith, L., & Whiteley, G. (2005). *The re-inventing schools implementation monitoring survey, Alaska benchmark/high school graduation qualifying examination data, and relationships between the two.* Anchorage, AK: Reinventing Schools Coalition.

Collins, L. M., & Sayer, A. G. (Eds.). (2001). *New methods for the analysis of change.* Washington, DC: American Psychological Association.

Covington, M. V. (1992). *Making the grade: A self-worth perspective on motivation and school reform.* New York: Cambridge University Press.

Covington, M. V., Omelich, C. L., & Schwarzer, R. (1986). Anxiety, aspirations, and self-concept in the achievement process: A longitudinal model with latent variables. *Motivation and Emotion, 10,* 71–88.

Crooks, T. J. (1988). The impact of classroom evaluation practices on students. *Review of Educational Research, 58*(4), 438–481.

Cross, K. P. (1998). Classroom research: Implementing the scholarship of teaching. In T. Angelo (Ed.), *Classroom assessment and research: An update on uses, approaches, and research findings* (pp. 5–12). San Francisco: Jossey-Bass.

Durm, M. W. (1993, Spring). An A is not an A is not an A: A history of grading. *The Educational Forum, 57,* 294–297.

Embretson, S. E., & Reise, S. P. (2000). *Item response theory for psychologists.* Mahwah, NJ: Erlbaum.

English, F. W. (2000). *Deciding what to teach and test: Developing, aligning, and auditing the curriculum.* Thousand Oaks, CA: Corwin Press.

Farkas, S., Friedman, W., Boese, J., & Shaw, G. (1994). *First things first: What Americans expect from public schools.* New York: Public Agenda.

Feldt, L. S., & Brennan, R. L. (1989). Reliability. In R. L. Linn (Ed.), *Educational measurement* (3rd ed., pp. 105–146). New York: Macmillan.

Fitts, P. M., & Posner, M. I. (1967). *Human performance.* Belmont, CA: Brooks/Cole.

Flicek, M. (2005a). Consistency of rubric scoring for common assessments for math that are a part of NCSD body of evidence (BoE) for high school graduation. *NCSD Assessment and Research Brief, 8,* 1–21.

Flicek, M. (2005b). Moving toward a valuable and reliable teacher judgment of student performance on standards. *NCSD Assessment and Research Brief, 4,* 1–3.

Frisbie, D. A. (2005). Measurement 101: Some fundamentals revisited. *Educational Measurement: Issues and Practice, 24*(3), 21–29.

Fuchs, L. S., & Fuchs, D. (1986). Effects of systematic formative evaluation: A meta analysis. *Exceptional Children, 53*(3), 199–208.

Gagne, R. M. (1977). *The conditions of learning* (3rd ed.). New York: Holt, Rinehart & Winston.

Gagne, R. M. (1989). *Studies of learning: 50 years of research.* Tallahassee: Florida State University, Learning Systems Institute.

Gentile, J. R., & Lalley, J. P. (2003). *Standards and mastery learning.* Thousand Oaks, CA: Corwin Press.

Glaser, R., & Linn, R. (1993). Foreword. In L. Shepard, *Setting performance standards for student achievement* (pp. xiii–xiv). Stanford, CA: National Academy of Education, Stanford University.

Glass, G. V. (1976). Primary, secondary, and meta-analyses. *Educational Researcher, 5,* 3–8.

Goodlad, J. I. (1984). *A place called school: Prospects for the future.* New York: McGraw-Hill.

Gulliksen, H. (1950). *Theory of mental tests.* New York: Wiley.

Guskey, T. R. (1980). What is mastery learning? *Instructor, 90*(3), 80–86.

Guskey, T. R. (1985). *Implementing mastery learning.* Belmont, CA: Wadsworth.

Guskey, T. R. (1987). Rethinking mastery learning reconsidered. *Review of Educational Research, 57,* 225–229.

Guskey, T. R. (Ed.). (1996a). *Communicating student learning* (1996 ASCD Yearbook). Alexandria, VA: Association for Supervision and Curriculum Development.

Guskey, T. R. (1996b). Reporting on student learning: Lessons from the past—Prescriptions for the future. In T. R. Guskey (Ed.), *Communicating student learning* (1996 ASCD Yearbook, pp. 13–24). Alexandria, VA: Association for Supervision and Curriculum Development.

Guskey, T. R., & Bailey, J. M. (2001). *Developing grading and reporting systems for student learning.* Thousand Oaks, CA: Corwin Press.

Haladyna, T. M. (1999). *A complete guide to student grading.* Boston: Allyn & Bacon.

Hambleton, R. K., Swaminathan, H., & Rogers, H. J. (1991). *Fundamentals of item response theory.* Newbury Park, CA: SAGE Publications.

Harrison, G. A., Weiner, J. S., Tanner, J. M., & Barnicot, N. A. (1964). *Human biology: An introduction to human evolution, variation, and growth.* London: Oxford University Press.

Hattie, J. (1984). An empirical study of various indices for determining unidimensionality. *Multivariate Behavioral Research, 19,* 49–78.

Hattie, J. (1985). Methodology review: Assessing the unidimensionality of tests and items. *Applied Psychological Measurement, 9*(2), 139–164.

Hattie, J. A. (1992). Measuring the effects of schooling. *Australian Journal of Education, 36*(1), 5–13.

Hattie, J., Krakowski, K., Rogers, H. J., & Swaminathan, H. (1996). An assessment of Stout's index of essential unidimensionality. *Applied Psychological Measurement, 20*(1), 1–14.

Haycock, K. (1998). Good teaching matters . . . a lot. *Thinking K–16, 3*(2), 1–14.

Hays, W. L. (1973). *Statistics for the social sciences.* (2nd ed.). New York: Holt, Rinehart, & Winston.

Kendall, J. (2000). Topics: A roadmap to standards. *NASSP Bulletin, 84*(620), 37–44.

Kendall, J. S., & Marzano, R. J. (2000). *Content knowledge: A compendium of standards and benchmarks for K–12 education* (3rd ed.). Alexandria, VA: Association for Supervision and Curriculum Development.

Kifer, E. (1994). Development of the Kentucky instructional results information system (KIRIS). In T. R. Guskey (Ed.), *High stakes performance assessment: Perspective on Kentucky's educational reform* (pp. 7–18). Thousand Oaks, CA: Corwin Press.

Kleinsasser, A. (1991, September). *Rethinking assessment: Who's the expert?* Paper presented at the Casper Outcomes Conference, Casper, WY.

Kluger, A. N., & DeNisi, A. (1996). The effects of feedback interventions on performance: A historical review, a meta-analysis and a preliminary intervention theory. *Psychological Bulletin, 119*(2), 254–284.

LaBerge, D., & Samuels, S. J. (1974). Toward a theory of automatic information processing in reading comprehension. *Cognitive Psychology, 6,* 293–323.

Lauer, P. A., Snow, D., Martin-Glenn, M., Van Buhler, R., Stoutemyer, K., & Snow-Renner, R. (2005). *The influence of standards on K–12 teaching and student learning.: A research synthesis.* Aurora, CO: Mid-continent Research for Education and Learning.

Lord, F. M. (1959, June). Problems in mental test theory arising from errors of measurement. *Journal of the American Statistical Association, 54*(286), 472–479.

Lord, F. M., & Novick, M. R. (1968). *Statistical theories of mental test scores.* Reading, MA: Addison-Wesley.

Lou, Y., Abrami, P. C., Spence, J. C., Poulsen, C., Chambers, B., & d'Appollonia, S. (1996). Within-class grouping: A meta-analysis. *Review of Educational Research, 66*(4), 423–458.

Magnusson, D. (1966). *Test theory.* Reading, MA: Addison-Wesley.

Marzano, R. J. (2000). *Transforming classroom grading.* Alexandria, VA: Association for Supervision and Curriculum Development.

Marzano, R. J. (2001). *Designing a new taxonomy of educational objectives.* Thousand Oaks, CA: Corwin Press.

Marzano, R. J. (2002a). A comparison of selected methods of scoring classroom assessments. *Applied Measurement in Education, 15*(3), 249–268.

Marzano, R. J. (2002b). *Identifying the primary instructional concepts in mathematics: A linguistic approach.* Centennial, CO: Marzano & Associates.

Marzano, R. J. (2003). *What works in schools: Translating research into action.* Alexandria, VA: Association for Supervision and Curriculum Development.

Marzano, R. J. (2004a). *Applying the theory on measurement of change to formative classroom assessments.* Centennial, CO: Marzano & Associates.

Marzano, R. J. (2004b). *Building background knowledge for academic achievement.* Alexandria, VA: Association for Supervision and Curriculum Development.

Marzano, R. J. (2004c). *Workshop materials.* Centennial, CO: Marzano & Associates.

Marzano, R. J. (2006). Unpublished data.

Marzano, R. J., & Haystead, M. (in press). *Making standards useful to classroom teachers.* Centennial, CO: Marzano & Associates.

Marzano, R. J., & Kendall, J. S. (1996). *A comprehensive guide to designing standards-based districts, schools, and classrooms.* Alexandria, VA: Association for Supervision and Curriculum Development.

Marzano, R. J., & Kendall, J. S. (in press). *The new taxonomy of educational objectives.* Thousand Oaks, CA: Corwin Press.

Marzano, R. J., Kendall, J. S., & Cicchinelli, L. F. (1998). *What Americans believe students should know: A survey of U.S. adults.* Aurora, CO: Mid-continent Research for Education and Learning.

Marzano, R. J., Kendall, J. S., & Gaddy, B. B. (1999). *Essential knowledge: The debate over what American students should know.* Aurora, CO: Mid-continent Research for Education and Learning.

Marzano, R. J., Marzano, J. S., & Pickering, D. J. (2003). *Classroom management that works: Research-based strategies for every teacher.* Alexandria, VA: Association for Supervision and Curriculum Development.

Marzano, R. J., Pickering, D. J., & Pollock, J. E. (2001). *Classroom instruction that works: Research-based strategies for increasing student achievement.* Alexandria, VA: Association for Supervision and Curriculum Development.

McMillan, J. H. (1997). *Classroom assessment: Principles and practices for effective instruction.* Needham Heights, MA: Allyn & Bacon.

McMillan, J. H. (2000). *Basic assessment concepts for teachers and administrators*. Thousand Oaks, CA: Corwin Press.

Mead, R., & Pike, D. J. (1975). A review of response surface methodology from a biometric viewpoint. *Biometrics, 31*, 803–851.

National Council of Teachers of Mathematics. (2000). *Principles and standards for school mathematics*. Reston, VA: Author.

National Education Goals Panel. (1991). *The National Education Goals report: Building a community of learners*. Washington, DC: Author.

National Education Goals Panel. (1993, November). *Promises to keep: Creating high standards for American students*. A report on the review of education standards from the Goal 3 and 4 Technical Planning Group to the National Education Goals Panel. Washington, DC: Author.

National Governors Association. (1996, March). *1996 National Education Summit policy statement*. Washington, DC: Author.

National Research Council. (1996). *National science education standards*. Washington, DC: National Academy Press.

Natriello, G. (1987). The impact of evaluation processes on students. *Educational Psychologist, 22*(2), 155–175.

Newell, A., & Rosenbloom, P. S. (1981). Mechanisms of skill acquisition and the law of practice. In J. R. Anderson (Ed.), *Cognitive skills and their acquisition*. Hillsdale, NJ: Erlbaum.

Nunally, J. C. (1967). *Psychometric theory*. New York: McGraw-Hill.

Nye, B., Konstantopoulos, S., & Hedges, L. V. (2004). How large are teacher effects? *Educational Evaluation and Policy Analysis, 26*(3), 237–257.

O'Connor, K. (1995). Guidelines for grading that support learning and success. *NASSP Bulletin, 79*(571), 91–101.

Ohio Department of Education. (2001). *Academic content standards: K–12 mathematics*. Columbus, OH: Author.

Olson, L. (1995, June 14). Cards on the table. *Education Week*, 23–28.

Osborne, J. W. (2003). Effect sizes and the disattenuation of correlation and regression coefficients: Lessons from educational psychology. *Practical Assessment, Research and Evaluation, 8*(11) [Online]. Retrieved December 29, 2003, from http://PAREonline.net/getvn.asp?v=8&n=11

Plake, B. S., Hambleton, R. K., & Jaeger, R. M. (1995). *A new standard-setting method for performance assessments: The dominant profile judgment method and some field test results*. Paper presented at the annual meeting of the American Educational Research Association, San Francisco.

Popham, W. J. (2003). *Test better, teach better: The instructional role of assessment*. Alexandria, VA: Association for Supervision and Curriculum Development.

Rasch, G. (1960). *Probabilistic models for some intelligence and attainment tests*. Chicago: University of Chicago Press.

Ravitch, D. (1983). *The troubled crusade: American education 1945–1980*. New York: Basic Books.

Reeves, D. B. (2002). *Holistic accountability: Serving students, schools, and community*. Thousand Oaks, CA: Corwin Press.

Reeves, D. B. (2004, December). The case against the zero. *Phi Delta Kappan, 86*(4), 324–325.

Rogosa, D. R., Brandt, D., & Zimowsky, M. (1982). A growth curve approach to the measurement of change. *Psychological Bulletin, 90*, 726–748.

Ross, J. A., Hogaboam-Gray, A., & Rolheiser, C. (2002). Student self-evaluation in grade 5–6 mathematics: Effects on problem-solving achievement. *Educational Assessment, 8*(1), 43–59.

Rothblum, E. D., Solomon, L. J., & Murakami, J. (1986). Affective, cognitive, and behavioral differences between high and low procrastinators. *Journal of Counseling Psychology, 33*, 387–394.

Rothman, R. (1995). The certificate of initial mastery. *Educational Leadership, 52*(8), 41–45.

Sanders, W. L., & Horn, S. P. (1994). The Tennessee value-added assessment system (TVAAS): Mixed-model methodology in educational assessment. *Journal of Personnel Evaluation in Education, 8*, 299–311.

Schmidt, W. H., McKnight, C. C., & Raizen, S. A. (1996). *Splintered vision: An investigation of U.S. science and mathematics education: Executive summary*. Lansing, MI: U.S. National Research Center for the Third International Mathematics and Science Study, Michigan State University.

Schreiber, R., & Battino, W. (2002). *A guide to reinventing schools.* Chugach, AK: Reinventing Schools Coalition.

Scriven, M. (1967). The methodology of evaluation. In R. F. Stake (Ed.), *Curriculum evaluation: American Educational Research Association monograph series on evaluation, No. 1* (pp. 39–83). Chicago: Rand McNally.

Secretary's Commission on Achieving Necessary Skills. (1991). *What work requires of schools: A SCANS report for America 2000.* Washington, DC: U.S. Department of Labor.

Seigel, D. G. (1975). Several approaches for measuring average rate of change for a second degree polynomial. *The American Statistician, 29,* 36–37.

Seligman, M. E. P. (1975). *Helplessness: On depression, development, and death.* San Francisco: Freeman.

Seligman, M. E. P., Maier, S. F., & Greer, J. (1968). The alleviation of learned helplessness in the dog. *Journal of Abnormal Psychology, 73,* 256–262.

Shadish, W. R., Cook, T. D., & Campbell, D. T. (2002). *Experimental and quasi-experimental designs for general causal inference.* Boston: Houghton Mifflin.

Smith, J. K., Smith, L. F., & DeLisi, R. (2001). *Natural classroom assessment.* Thousand Oaks, CA: Corwin Press.

Snow, R. E., & Lohman, D. F. (1989). Implications of cognitive psychology for educational measurement. In R. L. Linn (Ed.), *Educational measurement* (3rd ed., pp. 263–331). New York: American Council on Education and Macmillan.

Snyder, C. R. (1984, September). Excuses, excuses: They sometimes actually work to relieve the burden of blame. *Psychology Today, 18,* 50–55.

Solomon, L. J., & Rothblum, E. D. (1984). Academic procrastination: Frequency and cognitive-behavior correlates. *Journal of Counseling Psychology, 31,* 503–509.

Spady, W. G. (1988). Organizing for results: The basics of authentic restructuring and reform. *Educational Leadership, 46*(2), 4–8.

Spady, W. G. (1992). It's time to take a clear look at outcome-based education. *Outcome, 11*(2), 6–13.

Spady, W. G. (1994). Choosing outcomes of significance. *Educational Leadership, 51*(6), 18–22.

Spady, W. G. (1995). Outcome-based education: From instructional reform to paradigm restructuring. In H. H. Block, S. T. Everson, & T. Guskey (Eds.), *School improvement programs* (pp. 367–398). New York: Scholastic.

Stiggins, R. J. (1994). *Student-centered classroom assessment.* New York: Merrill.

Stiggins, R. J. (1997). *Student-centered classroom assessment* (2nd ed.). Columbus, OH: Merrill.

Stiggins, R. J., Arter, J. A., Chappuis, J., & Chappuis, S. (2004). *Classroom assessment for student learning.* Portland, OR: Assessment Training Institute.

Terwilliger, J. S. (1989, June). Classroom standard setting and grading practices. *Educational Measurement: Issues and Practice, 8*(2), 15–19.

Thorndike, E. L. (1904). *An introduction to the theory of mental and social measurement.* New York: Teachers College Press.

Tyack, D. K., & Tobin, W. (1994). The "grammar" of schooling: Why has it been so hard to change? *American Educational Research Journal, 31*(3), 453–479.

Valencia, S. W., Stallman, A. C., Commeyras, M., Pearson, P. D., & Hartman, D. K. (1991). Four measures of topical knowledge: A study of construct validity. *Reading Research Quarterly, 26*(3), 204–233.

Walberg, H. J. (1997). Uncompetitive American schools: Causes and cures. In *Brookings papers on educational policy, 1997.* Washington, DC: Brookings Institution.

Weiner, B. (1972). *Theories of motivation: From mechanism to cognition.* Chicago: Markham.

Weiner, B. (1974). *Achievement motivation and attribution theory.* Morristown, NJ: General Learning Press.

Weiner, B., Frieze, L., Kukla, A., Reed, L., Rest, S., & Rosenbaum, R. (1971). Perceiving the causes of success and failure. In E. E. Jones, D. E. Kanouse, H. H. Kelley, R. E. Nisbett, S. Valins, & B. Weiner (Eds.), *Attribution: Perceiving the causes of behavior* (pp. 95–121). Morristown, NJ: General Learning Press.

Wiggins, G., & McTighe, J. (2005). *Understanding by design (expanded 2nd ed).* Alexandria, VA: Association for Supervision and Curriculum Development.

Willett, J. B. (1985). *Investigating systematic individual difference in academic growth*. Unpublished doctoral dissertation, Stanford University, Palo Alto, CA.

Willett, J. B. (1988). Questions and answers in the measurement of change. *Review of Research in Education, 15*, 345–422. Washington, DC: American Educational Research Association.

Wilson, V. L., & Putnam, R. R. (1982). A meta-analysis of pretest sensitization effects on experimental design. *American Educational Research Journal, 19*(2), 249–258.

Wright, S. P., Horn, S. P., & Sanders, W. L. (1997). Teacher and classroom context effects on student achievement: Implications for teacher education. *Journal of Personnel Evaluation in Education, 11*, 57–67.

INDEX

Page numbers followed by f indicate reference to a figure.

Covington, Martin, 7, 89
Crooks, Terrance, 9
Cross, K. Patricia, 92–93

data analysis software, 105–112,
    135
decision making, measuring
    knowledge with, 73*f*
DeLisi, Richard, 32
DeLorenzo, Richard, 141
demonstrations, 82, 85
DeNisi, Angelo, 6–7
diagnostic learning log, 93–94
difference score function,
    158–159
discussion, impromptu, 81–82
districts, transforming
    the culture in, 132–136,
    140–143
drive theory, 7–8
Durm, Mark, 79

education, transforming the
    culture of, 136–143, 141*f*,
    142*f*
effect size, 144
Embretson, Susan, 37–38, 149
English, Fenwick, 14
error analysis, measuring
    knowledge with, 68*f*, 69
error score, 36–37, 94–96, 95*f*
essays, measuring knowledge
    with, 79–80
evaluation, defined, 35
Excelsior, Pinnacle Plus
    software, 106–112, 107*f*,
    109*f*, 112*f*, 113*f*, 133
exercises, measuring knowledge
    with, 71–72
experimental inquiry, measuring
    knowledge with, 73*f*

Farkas, S., 25
feedback, achievement and,
    5–8, 5*f*
Feldt, L. S., 160
First Things First (Farkas,
    Friedman, Boese, & Shaw),
    25
forced-choice items and tasks,
    76, 77–78*f*
Friedman, W., 25

Frisbie, David, 53, 150–152,
    157, 158
Fuchs, Douglas, 5, 10
Fuchs, Lynn, 5, 10

Gainer, L. J., 25
Gaussian distribution, 150
generalization, measuring
    knowledge with, 65, 67, 67*f*
Gentile, J. Ronald, 137
Germany, 13
Glaser, Robert, 12
Glass, Carl Friedrich, 150
Glass, G. V., 144
Goodlad, John, 139
grade books, 100–103, 100*f*, 133
grade level organization,
    138–139
grade point average (GPA), on
    report cards, 126
grades. *See also* report cards
    certificates of mastery and,
        27, 140
    compensatory system,
        120–122, 120*f*, 121*f*, 123
    conjunctive approach,
        123–124, 124*f*
    cutoff points, 122–123
    final, 119–124, 120*f*, 121*f*
    translating scores to,
        122–124
    weighting role in, 120–122,
        120*f*, 121*f*
grading systems, selecting,
    135
growth functions
    difference score, 158–161
    multiwave linear, 161–164
A Guide to Reinventing Schools
    (Schreiber & Battino), 140
Guskey, Thomas, 103, 115,
    122

Hambleton, R. K., 148
Harrison, Geoffrey, 150
Hattie, John, 5, 14, 146–147
Haycock, Kati, 2
Hays, W. L., 154
High School (Boyer), 138
high school measurement
    topics, 26–27, 134
Horn, Sandra, 1

IF-THEN structures, 70, 74
illogical response patterns, 53,
    85–86
inferences, measuring
    knowledge with, 68–69,
    73–74
information, items or tasks
    measuring
    analogies, 68*f*, 69
    applications not taught in
        class, 68–69
    basic details, 65, 66*f*
    classifying, 68, 68*f*
    cognitive processes used in
        Type III, 68–69, 68*f*
    comparing, 68, 68*f*
    error analysis, 68*f*, 69
    essays, 80
    example, 64–65, 83–85
    forms of assessment
        matched to, 83*f*
    generalizations, 65, 67, 67*f*
    inferences not taught in
        class, 68–69
    metaphors, 68*f*, 69
    principles, 65, 67, 67*f*
    short written response,
        78–79
intelligence, artificial, 70
invention, measuring knowledge
    with, 73*f*
investigation, measuring
    knowledge with, 73*f*
IRT (item response theory), 37–38
IRT assessment model, 38–40,
    39*f*, 149
item, defined, 62. *See also* tasks
    and items

Japan, 13
joint scoring, 61–62, 119

Kendall, John, 16–17
Kluger, Avraham, 6–7
knowledge. *See also* information;
    mental procedures
    content vs. process, 70
    declarative, 64–70
    physical, 75
    procedural, 70
    psychomotor procedures,
        70–71, 74–75, 82, 83*f*,
        85–86

ABOUT THE AUTHOR

Robert J. Marzano is a Senior Scholar at Mid-continent Research for Education and Learning (McREL) in Aurora, Colorado; an Associate Professor at Cardinal Stritch University in Milwaukee, Wisconsin; and President of Marzano & Associates. He has developed programs and practices used in K–12 classrooms that translate current research and theory in cognition into instructional methods. An internationally known trainer and speaker, Marzano has authored 24 books and more than 150 articles and chapters in books on such topics as reading and writing instruction, thinking skills, school effectiveness, restructuring, assessment, cognition, and standards implementation. Recent titles include *School Leadership That Works: From Research to Results* (ASCD, 2005), *Building Background Knowledge for Academic Achievement: Research on What Works in Schools* (ASCD, 2004); *Classroom Management That Works: Research-Based Strategies for Every Teacher* (ASCD, 2003); *What Works in Schools: Translating Research into Action* (ASCD, 2003); *Classroom Instruction That Works: Research Strategies for Increasing Student Achievement* (ASCD, 2001); *Designing a New Taxonomy of Educational Objectives* (Corwin, 2001). Marzano received his bachelor's degree in English from Iona College in New York, a master's degree in education in reading/language arts from Seattle University, and a doctorate in curriculum and instruction from the University of Washington. Address: 7127 S. Danube Court, Centennial, CO 80016 USA. Telephone: (303) 796-7683. E-mail: robertjmarzano@aol.com

Related Resources

Use Excelsior Software's Pinnacle Plus™ for recording and tracking student performance—a key factor in What Works in Schools. To learn more, visit www.excelsiorsoftware.com

At the time of publication, the following ASCD resources were available; for the most up-to-date information about ASCD resources, go to www.ascd.org. ASCD stock numbers are noted in parentheses.

Networks
Visit the ASCD Web site (www.ascd.org) and search for "networks" for information about professional educators who have formed groups around topics such as "Arts in Education," "Authentic Assessment," and "Brain-Based Compatible Learning." Look in the "Network Directory" for current facilitators' addresses and phone numbers.

Online Course
What Works in Schools: An Introduction by John Brown (#PD04OC36)

Print Products
Building Background Knowledge for Academic Achievement: Research on What Works in Schools by Robert J. Marzano (#104017)

Classroom Instruction That Works: Research-Based Strategies for Increasing Student Achievement by Robert J. Marzano, Debra J. Pickering, Jane E. Pollock (#101010)

Classroom Management That Works: Research Based Strategies for Every Teacher by Robert J. Marzano, Jana S. Marzano, Debra J. Pickering (#103027)

Grading and Reporting Student Learning by Robert J. Marzano and Tom Guskey (Professional Inquiry Kit) (#901061)

A Handbook for Classroom Instruction That Works by Robert J. Marzano, Jennifer S. Norford, Diane E. Paynter, Debra J. Pickering, Barbara B. Gaddy (#101041)

A Handbook for Classroom Management That Works by Robert J. Marzano, Jana S. Marzano, Barbara B. Gaddy, Maria C. Foseid, Mark P. Foseid (#105012)

School Leadership That Works: From Research to Results by Robert J. Marzano, Timothy Waters, and Brian A. McNulty (#105125)

What Works in Schools: Translating Research into Practice by Robert J. Marzano (#102271)

Videotapes
Classroom Management That Works: Sharing Rules and Procedures (Tape 1, #404039)
Classroom Management That Works: Developing Relationships (Tape 2; #404040)
Classroom Management That Works: Fostering Student Self-Management (Tape 3; #404041)
What Works in Schools: School-Level Factors with Robert J. Marzano (Tape 1; # 403048)
What Works in Schools: Teacher-Level Factors with Robert J. Marzano (Tape 2; #403049)
What Works in Schools: Student-Level Factors with Robert J. Marzano (Tape 3; #403050)

For more information, visit us on the World Wide Web (http://www.ascd.org), send an e-mail message to member@ascd.org, call the ASCD Service Center (1-800-933-ASCD or 703-578-9600, then press 2), send a fax to 703-575-5400, or write to Information Services, ASCD, 1703 N. Beauregard St., Alexandria, VA 22311-1714 USA.